# THE
# STREAMLINED DECADE

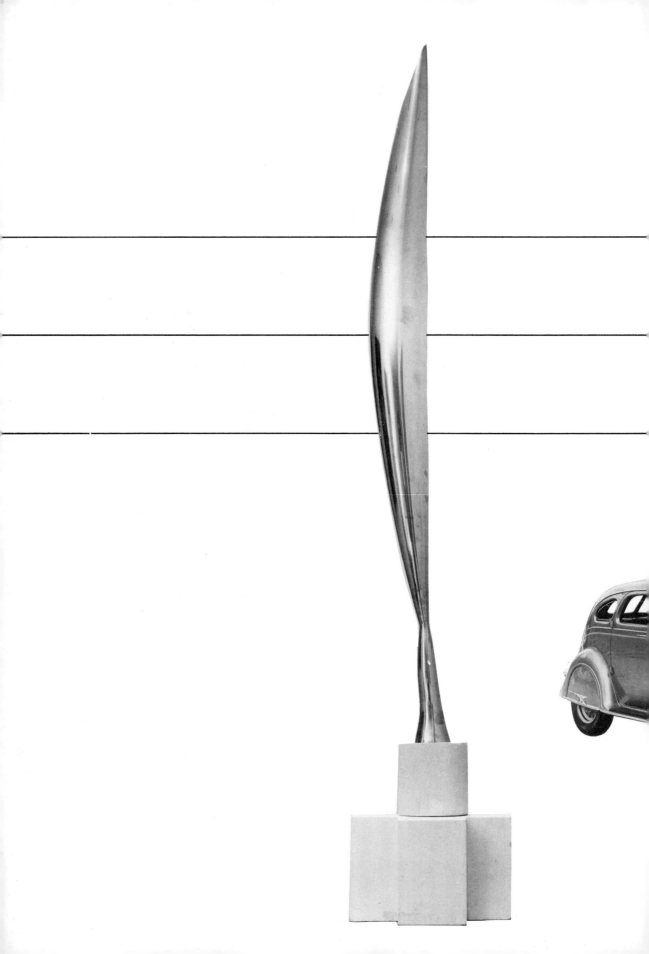

# THE STREAMLINED DECADE

Donald J. Bush

GEORGE BRAZILLER · NEW YORK

To my wife, Catharine, for her encouragement and support and for count-less hours of typing and reading the final manuscript.

To Dr. Peter Walch and Dean Clinton Adams of the University of New Mexico for their interest and guidance in the research and to Tom Barrow, Charles Mattox and Don Schlegel, also of the University of New Mexico, for many helpful suggestions.

Finally to Frank Malina, editor-publisher of *Leonardo,* for his en-thusiasm and advice while publishing excerpts from an earlier draft of this study.

*For information address the publisher:*
*George Braziller, Inc., One Park Avenue, New York 10016*

*Library of Congress Catalog Card Number: 75–10868*
*International Standard Book Number: 0–8076–0792–4, cloth*
*0–8076–0793–2, paper*

*Printed in the U.S.A.*
*First printing*
*Designed by The Etheredges*

For Catharine

# CONTENTS

# THE
# STREAMLINED DECADE

# I.
# INTRODUCTION

The desire to perform actions quickly, easily and without disruptions is a twentieth-century phenomenon evident in advanced-technology countries, especially the United States. It is manifest both in processes and in objects. One can cite such diverse examples as industrial time-motion studies, the superhighway system and the modern compact kitchen. "Streamlining," a term with origins in science, has become commonplace in our language. It is synonymous with saving time and energy, and streamlined forms are emblematic of speed and efficiency. These forms are usually characterized by rounded edges, smooth surfaces and low horizontal profiles. All are simplified by the design principle of *absorption*, the merging of one sub-form into another with transitional curves, and *reductivism*, the elimination of extraneous details. The resultant forms are intended to penetrate air or water with the least resistance. They contrast with angular geometric forms and tend to resemble the organic forms in nature. Indeed, natural forms, like fish and birds, suggested low-resistance forms to the scientists who pioneered hydrodynamics and aerodynamics.

Man-made streamlined designs, then, facilitate processes. The

1

streamlined vehicle makes travel faster or more efficient. The superhighway eliminates the disruptions of intersections; its gradual transitional curves allow drivers to transfer from one system to another and its ramps afford entry and exit—all with minimal loss of time.[1] The well-arranged modern kitchen saves steps and its rounded corners and smooth continuous working surfaces facilitate cleaning. In each of these examples, the intention is to provide forms that serve continuous activities with the least effort and the fewest stoppages. The streamlined form can be seen as an example of functional design. This book documents the development of a new *dynamic* functionalism evolved from scientific principles and incorporated into the design of vehicles, buildings and a variety of product designs in America during the period from the recession of 1927 to the beginning of the Second World War.

The story is seen against the background of the economic upheaval of the 1930s. It was a period of national disillusionment and confusion, one that called for dramatic solutions. Out of this came a new profession in America—industrial design. The first designers were drawn from advertising and theatrical designing for there was no formal training available to prepare artists for this new profession. Their earliest assignments involved the restyling of products and packaging in order to improve sagging sales figures. They acclimated to the industrial setting and eventually suggested technical innovations that improved product performance. With this added technical understanding and their experience in the commercial world they assumed the role of coordinating designers working with engineers, market analysts and sales managers. Raymond Loewy, Norman Bel Geddes, Henry Dreyfuss, Walter Dorwin Teague and others developed a reputation for solving problems large and small. This they accomplished with considerable flair and with the aid of their own staffs of specialists.

The imaginations and energies of these men led them beyond the designing of automobiles, radios and hundreds of other products that needed modernization. Like the significant architects of this century, the designers recognized the need for widespread and rational planning and the utilization of new scientific and technological advances. In the darkest days of the Depression they dreamed of orderly, hygienic cities and houses, ideal environments free of drudgery and fitted with material conveniences. They looked ahead to safe, fast travel on luxurious streamlined aircraft, trains, buses, ships and automobiles. Unlike modern architects, whose utopias rarely develop beyond the drawing stage, the first American industrial designers were able to build their model city, the 1939 New York World's Fair.

In retrospect we recognize that technology is a mixed blessing and we no longer assure ourselves that material comforts and harmonious surroundings guarantee well-ordered and contented societies. During the Depression, however, technology offered hope for solutions to problems of housing, transportation, agriculture and employment. In the stagnant economy of the decade, "getting things moving again" was a common desire expressed vicariously in transportation. Accordingly the design of vehicles advanced to a new stage as they became lower, sleeker and faster. The streamlined form came to symbolize progress and the promise of a better future. The optimism it—and its creators, the industrial designers—engendered was sorely needed in the decade following the market crash of 1929.

This volume is not an exhaustive catalogue of streamlined designs of the 1930s but offers a representative view of the range of applications of streamlining, its development from the sciences and its relationship to modern sculpture. The innumerable streamlined racing cars and planes are not considered for they are already documented and their influence upon vehicle design is obvious. Instead, the intention is to recreate the distinctive appearance of things in a unique era and hopefully some of the excitement that attended their original appearances. From the beginning, the streamlined form had its detractors among reactionaries as well as modernists who adhered to alternate functionalist theories.[2] Widely and unwisely applied by lesser artists than those discussed here, streamlining fell into disrepute. By the late 1940s, it had come to denote a bloated, chromium-covered teardrop that housed a clock, a vacuum or perhaps, in wretched excess, a music box, cigarettes or nonpareils.[3] Even the pioneer designers, at last established in a respectable profession, disavowed streamlining. A reexamination of the serious designs of the Streamlined Decade, however, reveals a number of handsome and exciting forms and the origins of a new aesthetic of uncluttered sculptural organic forms.[4] Finally, the designs and the story of their creation provide an additional dimension to the 1930s that helps to explain the mood of a nation and the interests of its citizens in times of great duress.

# II.
# THE /CIENCE OF PENETRATION

## THE TRUE FORM OF LEAST RESISTANCE

The roots of streamlining as a design principle are to be found in the history of hydrodynamics and aerodynamics. Daniel Bernoulli introduced the term *hydrodynamics* to encompass the sciences of hydrostatics and hydraulics. He published his first book on the subject in 1738.[1] However, until empirical data could be assembled, hull designs were still based on intuition and trial and error. Crude experiments providing data were reported in England as early as 1765, and it is probable that similar efforts were being made in France. A proposal in 1869 to tow one of Her Majesty's ships in "sheltered waters" in order to measure speed and resistance was rejected by the British Admiralty. Instead, they funded the experiments of Frederick Reech, who towed a variety of model hulls through a water-filled trench.[2]

It was determined in the nineteenth century that the motion of fluids takes place under two forms, laminar and turbulent flow (fig. 1). Laminar flow can be envisioned as a series of parallel layers in a moving fluid, each having its own velocity and direction without disturbances in its forward motion. Turbulent flow is characterized by eddy currents or vortices, a tumbling of the fluid caused by an alien form. This turbulence creates a partial vacuum behind the form, which retards its forward progress.

When a body immersed in the flow does not induce turbulence, it may be said to be streamlined.[3] W. J. Macquorn Rankine is credited with the first theoretical drawings of streamlines, lines which represent typical parallel layers in a fluid surrounding a body.[4] Eventually these were visualized by flowing streams of smoke around models in wind tunnels.

In his first paper on aeronautics in 1804, Sir George Cayley proposed for the dirigible "a form approaching to that of a very oblong spheroid, but varied according to what may be found the true solid of least resistance in air," by which he meant an ideal streamlined body.[5] That general form would serve either in the sea or in the sky for both are fluid mediums. He turned his attention to nature, which had evolved efficient forms for swimming and flying. In 1809 he measured the girth of a trout at regular intervals along its length and converted these figures to mean

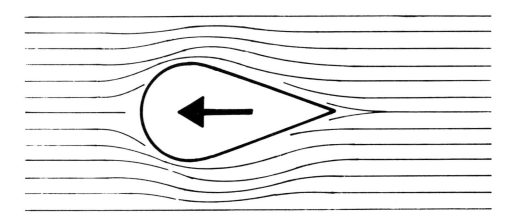

1. An approximation of the effects created in a flow by a streamlined body (ABOVE) and a nonstreamlined body (BELOW). (*Author's Collection.*)

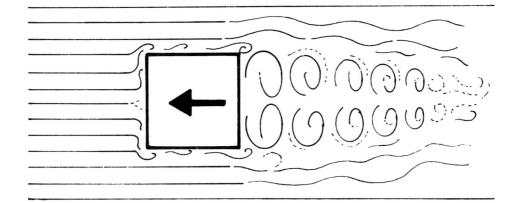

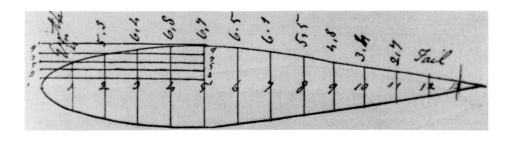

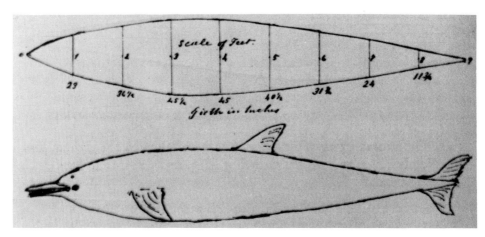

2.   Sir George Cayley. True Forms of Least Resistance. 1809 and later. (*Courtesy Charles H. Gibbs-Smith.*)

diameters. From these dimensions he whittled a wooden spindle symmetrical about its axis (fig. 2). Split lengthwise, he thought, the spindle would produce two ideal hulls. "We should then," he wrote, "be deriving our boat from a better architect than man, and should probably have the real solid of least resistance." [6]

By looking to nature for a solution, Cayley paid homage to *teleology,* the philosophy that finds evidence of design or purpose in nature. Later spindles were based on dolphins and woodcocks. He affirmed in 1810 that the shape of the trailing end of a body was as important in diminishing resistance as the front end, correctly assuming that the pressure in turbulent fluids is lower and tends to hold back the moving form. [7]

Wind tunnels were vital in the development of streamlined or low-resistance forms and of airfoils. The first wind tunnel was designed by Francis Wenham and installed at Greenwich, England in 1871. [8] Scientific data was gathered in several countries on hundreds of spindles, airfoils and even stuffed birds. The young science of photography was enlisted in the recording of laminar and turbulent flow around wind-tunnel models. Ludwig Mach used silk threads, cigarette smoke and glowing particles of hot iron to trace air patterns onto his plates. [9] Etienne Jules Marey analyzed the flight of birds, making photographs, drawings and bronze sculptures to visualize, in serial order, bodies at different points in time and space.[10] In 1899 he began to photograph smoke streams in wind tunnels.[11]

Animal locomotion was also the primary concern of Eadweard Muybridge, whose multiple photographs led to the development of motion pictures. In America, Thomas Eakins captured several views of an athlete on the first multiple-exposure plate. Frank Gilbreth analyzed the activities of workers and used wire sculpture to visualize their patterns, thereby initiating the time-motion and fatigue studies that we identify with the "efficiency expert." Thus the attention of pioneer investigators of aerodynamics, photography and animal locomotion coincided, in the late nineteenth century, in the study of efficient motion.[12]

An observer in the American Civil War, Count Ferdinand von Zeppelin, noted the use of tethered observer balloons and concluded that they ought to be made "dirigible," that is, powered and steered craft.[13] Early dirigibles, like those with which the dapper Alberto Santos-Dumont awed Paris, were nonrigid and depended upon internal pressure to maintain their form.[14] As early as 1896 the wind tunnel was used to gather data on the stability and critical speed of airships; the tests were conducted by Col. Charles Renard, constructor of the airship *La France*.[15]

The rigid-frame airship was developed in Germany where the first of this type was tested in 1897.[16] Zeppelin improved the type considerably, so much so that his name is for most people a synonym for airship. The cigar-shaped dirigibles soon captured the popular imagination (fig. 3).[17]

3. The Navy Rigid Airship *Los Angeles* (ZR–3). 1926. (*Official U.S. Navy photo.*)

4.  Artist's conception of a submarine. (*Official U.S. Navy photo.*)

That curiosity turned to fear when the Zeppelins, which in 1917 grew to seven-hundred and fifty feet in length and eighty feet in diameter, were used in aerial attacks upon London. A very similar form, the submarine, became a vehicle for terror in the Great War (fig. 4). Both airships and submarines were tapered cylinders designed for ease of penetration and minimal turbulence in their wake. Both operated totally immersed in their fluid environment with similar apparatus for climbing, diving and stabilizing against roll. Moving silently under the dark of night or in the mantle of ocean, these forms of least resistance made an indelible impression on the twentieth-century mind.

## STREAMLINING IN NATURE

Engineers have altered rigid forms moving in a particular medium for maximum speed and efficiency, according to the characteristics or requirements to be met. Whether optimizing for maximum speed, range or maneuverability, the engineer assists and directs the evolution of machines. So Darwinian in our outlook are we that we speak of "generations" of hardware adapted to their environmental demands.

In the natural sciences, the view is often taken that animal forms are altered directly by the forces upon them or more gradually by adaptation. In his classic treatise *On Growth and Form,* Sir D'Arcy Wentworth

Thompson used the term *streamlined* to describe organic structures that offer the least resistance while in motion. One example he used was the hen's egg. Its particular shape results from the deformation of an elastic spheroid in passing through a peristaltic tube (one in which motion is induced by progressive waves of contraction and relaxation). While in the oviduct, the egg may be viewed as "a stationary body round which waves are flowing, with the same result as when a body moves through a fluid at rest." [18] Thompson treated the development of the egg as a hydrodynamic problem, simplified by the absence of turbulence. It is a streamlined structure of a simple kind.

Thompson supported his thesis with a precise description of the formation of the egg and mathematical analysis of its form, combining biology with physics and mathematics. For Thompson, *organic design* was the result of applying nature's principles for greatest "mechanical efficiency":

> The naval architect learns a great part of his lesson from the stream-lining of a fish; the yachtsman learns that his sails are nothing more than a great bird's wing, causing the slender hull to fly along; and the mathematical study of the streamlines of a bird, and of the principles underlying the areas and curvatures of its wings and tail, has helped to lay the very foundations of the modern science of aeronautics.[19]

Moving freely from examples in nature to others in engineering, Thompson felt that man had discovered basic principles which had informed the natural process of adaptation. From hydrodynamics and aerodynamics we learn "the enormous, the paramount importance" of streamlining. There would be no need for streamlining in a perfect fluid, but in water or air, the least imperfection in a streamlined body leads to pockets of dead water or dead air which spell high resistance and wasted energy.[20]

To solve the problem of how streamlined natural forms came to be, Thompson applied the principle of least action, the *loi de repos* which explains that a fluid medium tends to impress its stream-lines upon a deformable body until it yields and offers a minimum of resistance. Observation was his method; every form is a "diagram of forces" from which one can judge or deduce the forces that have acted upon it.[21] The evidence was to be found both in organic and inorganic forms:

> The contours of a snowdrift, of a windswept sand-dune, even of the flame of a lamp, show endless illustrations of stream-lines or eddy curves which the stream itself imposes, and which are oftentimes of

*great elegance and complexity. Always the stream tends to mold the bodies it streams over, facilitating its own flow; and the same principle must somehow come into play, at least as a contributory factor, in the making of a fish or of a bird.*[22]

## BIOMORPHIC SCULPTURE

D'Arcy Thompson's first edition of *On Growth and Form* in 1917 was contemporary with the appearance of abstracted symbols of speed and penetration sculpted by the Rumanian, Constantin Brancusi. In keeping with the dominant trend of twentieth-century art, reductivism, Brancusi distilled his experience of nature to simple forms:

*The egg . . . takes on its ovoid shape by virtue of the mechanical forces which operate during its growth, gestation and delivery. When Brancusi conceived a symbol in marble for* The Beginning of the World *(1924), it assumed an egg shape. This was perhaps a reduction of the process of art to an imitation of natural processes. . . .*[23]

Thus Herbert Read described how Brancusi's work exemplified the ideal of universal harmony, which implies that form is determined by physical laws in the process of growth. The egg was in fact the end-product of an eighteen-year evolution of a single theme that had begun in 1906 with his *Sleeping Muse,* an impressionistic head emerging from a mass of stone, and continued with a second version, an isolated ovoid with features bearing comparison with cubist sculpture. By 1911, in *Prometheus,* the head had assumed a more pronounced teardrop shape. *Newborn* of 1915 is less elongated and has facets representing the wailing mouth and brow of an infant. With *The Beginning of the World,* the reductive process was complete; the artist had removed successive layers to arrive at the "form-core." [24] This ovoid was at once the simplest and the most fundamental and universal form.

Brancusi's mature works are of two types: the purified and polished organic forms in bronze or marble and the rougher works in wood and stone that relate to the "primitive" sources in modern art. Like primitive art these latter images are symbolic, but one of them, the *Endless Column* of 1918, is, despite its handwrought finish, an allusion to modern production. Along a length of timber Brancusi repeated a geometric module whose width, length and height are in the ratio 1:2:4. This rationalization of proportions and the sense of systematic, continuous extension suggest the standardization, formulation and repetition typical of the modern assembly line.

The high finish of Brancusi's polished bronzes recalls the machine aesthetic that emerged from the Bauhaus, yet the perfection of these surfaces could be attained only by exquisite hand-craftsmanship. Isamu Noguchi, once his assistant, recalled Brancusi's dissatisfaction with a metal disk that had been machine-polished in Germany.[25] Despite its organic form and hand finish, *Bird in Space* (1943—fig. 5) continues to be compared with propellers, torpedoes and rockets as though it alluded to modern technology. Athena Spear reminds us that the first in the *Bird* series (1919) was developed between the World Wars, a formative period in modern ballistics.[26]

It was the concept of flight rather than the mechanics of flight that interested Brancusi, and he fused his concept with the vital form of the bird. *Bird in Space* is an essence removed from the confusions and irrelevancies of nature. His sculptural program paralleled the technique of the modern scientist who isolates a phenomenon and controls variables in order to approach a fundamental truth. In the several *Fish*, Brancusi recognized the functional quality of the creature and its seemingly effortless motion. His purified versions are without detail and are not unlike Cayley's "true form of least resistance." These hydrodynamical ideal forms are expressive of the *élan vital* in nature.

> . . . *when you see a fish, you do not think of its scales, do you? You think of its floating, flashing body seen through water. . . . Well, I've tried to express just that. If I made fins and eyes and scales, I would arrest its movement and hold you by a pattern, or a shape of reality. I want just the flash of its spirit.*[27]

Brancusi's understanding of nature was spiritual rather than scientific, and he sought to express the spirit of each creature in a refined, abstracted form. His interest in birds, eggs, fish, seals (fig. 6) and penguins was shared by D'Arcy Thompson, his contemporary. Each recognized the dynamic functional qualities in creatures and expressed them in his own way; Brancusi in polished bronze or marble and Thompson with mathematics. Jean Arp, Barbara Hepworth, Henry Moore and others created monumental and vitalistic organic sculpture but rarely with a sense of movement through space. Others preferred to depict chaotic mechano-organic motion, as in the staccato pulsing of Jacob Epstein's ominous *Rock Drill* of 1913. In Boccioni's *Unique Forms of Continuity in Space* (fig. 7), the figure struggles forward in baroque swirls of drapery that define the turbulence in his wake. It is the exact opposite of Brancusi's creatures, which are lively and graceful. In them a designer wishing to develop forms

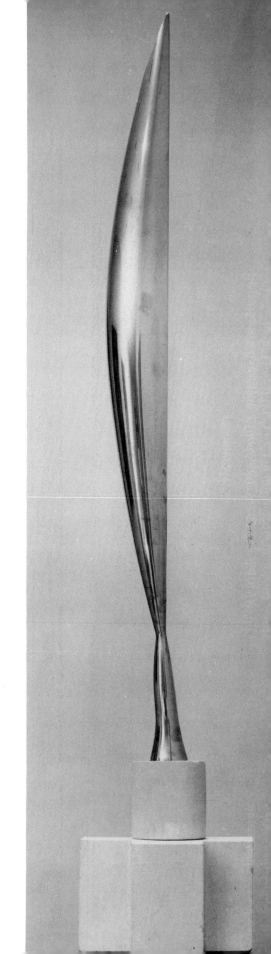

5. Constantin Brancusi. *Bird in Space*. 1943. (*Collection, The Museum of Modern Art, New York, Gift of Mr. and Mrs. William A. M. Burden, Donor retaining life interest.*)

6. Constantin Brancusi. *White Seal (Miracle)*. Ca. 1936. (*The Solomon R. Guggenheim Museum.*)

7.   Umberto Boccioni. *Unique Forms of Continuity in Space.* 1913. (*The Museum of Modern Art, New York. Acquired through the Lillie P. Bliss Bequest.*)

symbolizing ease of penetration and swift motion could find ample inspiration.

The most cursory review of popular scientific and popular mechanic magazines or the pulp magazines of the first three decades of this century will turn up dozens of streamlined ships, submarines, airplanes and airships, high-speed trains and teardrop autos. Speculation was rampant and artists were kept busy supplying the Sunday supplements with visual conceptions of a future New York over which hovered Zeppelins bound for Europe, Japan, the Panama Canal and the South Pole. The possibilities for aerodynamics seemed endless and encouraged projections of nearly instantaneous global travel, of mammoth vehicles conveying travelers at low cost in high style, and of multideck cities with a hierarchy of subways, streetcars, elevated monorails, rooftop landing strips and airships.

All the while, scientists gathered data and developed formulae that would make aerodynamics a more sophisticated, more complex science. In the long run, they would become the skeptics, able to demonstrate mathematically the limitations of streamlining. As we shall see, the enthusiasm did not wane until the very late 1930s and not until many a backyard inventor had shrouded his Model T in the semblance of a "teardrop" (a shape that proved to be mythical itself!) and had gotten his picture in *Popular Mechanics*.

Streamlining vied for attention with radio, television and telescopes but profited from the excitement that these and other scientific devices aroused. As the term *streamlining* gained currency, it became more than a technique; it became a viewpoint. Biologists could examine nature for evidence of streamlining and sculptors could express the spirit of *élan vital* in creatures studied by those biologists. It remained for industrial designers to promote streamlining as a symbol that touched our daily lives.

# III.
# IDEAL FORMS

## THE PREHISTORY OF AMERICAN INDUSTRIAL DESIGN

Until the late nineteen-twenties "art in industry" referred to the design of minor arts—such traditional artifacts of applied art as furniture, dishware, crystal, silver, textiles, carpets and wallpapers. The industrial artist with some beaux-arts or technical-vocational schooling in pattern designing, stencil-cutting and the vocabulary of ornament created decor suited to a variety of tastes. Smart shops often engaged their own designers and manufacturers to create exclusive, expensive and elegant *objets d'art*. Under the spell of the new wave of modernism radiating from Paris, the limited-edition object featured a soberness of ornament and a dependence upon effects produced by proportion and a richness of materials.[1]

At the other extreme were the mass-produced goods stamped from machines or cast in molds and rushed past the brushes of a dozen artists who, upon command, could paint miniature roses or the red lips, blue eyes and rosy cheeks of peasant children. Here "applied art" had a literal meaning, and when the demand for what was variously called *La Mode 1925*, *Modernistic* and *Jazz Moderne* was felt in the neighborhood department store or five-and-dime, the rosebud stencils were stored and new ones were cut in the shape of lightning bolts, sunrays, fountains and other Art Deco motifs.[2] Elongated and languid Pierrots and Pierrettes displaced the shepherds and milkmaidens. Cathedral radios were replaced with stair-stepped angular versions rising from their stands like small skyscrapers.

That automobiles, telephones and refrigerators could become works of art had not yet occurred to most Americans. Perhaps it was difficult to see beyond their functions or the conveniences they represented. The kitchen was a work place, not the combination laundry, wet bar and quick-food dispensing communications center it has since become. Behind swinging doors, kitchens were "a porcelain and surgical white," and as antiseptic as a hospital.[3] The modern house was "a biological institution" where the processes of hygiene and sanitation were to be facilitated.[4] Beauty was not yet a major factor in promoting kitchen equipment and bathroom fixtures; ease of maintenance and reliable performance were more significant than style.

The American automobile continued to be black and boxy until the New York Motor Show of 1926, where hard and brilliant new pyroxylin paints were introduced. One could now choose from Florentine Cream, Versailles Violet, Wedgewood Green and other colors with historical references.[5] More startling and portentous was the introduction the following year of a *styled* mass-produced auto bearing the name of the industrial giant who had once said he would not give five cents for all the art the world had produced.

The 1927 Model A signified no sudden aesthetic interest on the part of Henry Ford; it represented a necessary economic decision. Ford's own revolutionary methods and philosophy had spread to many industries making goods more abundant and less expensive, opening new markets and encouraging innovation. The buyer, conditioned to the novelty of changing fashions in clothing and interiors, could no longer be satisfied with the merely functional Model T for it had no "style."

## THE LULL BEFORE THE STORM

The phenomenal blossoming of the economy during the twenties was due in part to untrammeled speculation in the stock market and in part to a sharp increase in productivity. As a result of overproduction, the market for goods was becoming saturated, and 1927 saw a recession begin. Aware of the current interest in modern styles and motifs induced by the Paris Exposition two years earlier, manufacturers turned to their advertising agencies for advice on facelifting their goods. The agencies contacted the artists close at hand: advertising illustrators, graphic designers, package designers, window-display specialists and theatrical designers. They represented the fields in which the temporary nature of the finished product and its subjection to popular taste, fashion and commercial success were understood and accepted. It was natural, then, that the early efforts of the first generation of American industrial designers would concentrate on appearance rather than performance.

In practice the modern industrial designer must be concerned with both the appearance and the performance of his designs, so he calls upon the services of market analysts, engineers, sociologists and a host of other specialists. Given the responsibility to stimulate sales, the first designers repackaged their clients' products without such support. Remarkable successes gave the new profession a degree of authority. Raymond Loewy, for example, increased the sales of a radio seven-fold by restyling the cabinet. As the designers became more familiar with the machines and processes of industry they began to make suggestions leading to improvements in product performance and in assembly and construction techniques. When the Depression came and personal incomes dropped, their services were even more urgently required.

## ENTER THE DESIGNERS

The first office to offer industrial design services with the support of a varied staff of specialists was established by the successful poster artist and theatrical designer Norman Bel Geddes. Where other artists had served industry with, he felt, condescension, he saw such service as an opportunity. In 1927 he decided to experiment in designing motor cars, ships, factories and railways, things "more vitally akin to life today than the theatre." [7] Geddes was no stranger to technology, having introduced several technical innovations in theatrical lighting and sound effects, produced 35-mm films and invented an electric game.

With a talent for flamboyant gestures, Geddes established the early image of the industrial designer as one interested in solving any design problem and, in so doing, making earlier products and processes obsolete. *Fortune* described him in 1934 as a "bomb thrower" whose advanced designs would cost American industry a billion dollars in retooling.[8] When they were not occupied with their clients' products, Geddes assigned his staff of twenty engineers, architects and draftsmen to "development work" —imaginative exercises free of the limitations of cost but based on the needs of people, the laws of physics and feasible engineering practice. From this free-style collaboration came Geddes's first book, *Horizons* (1932) and "the design of ovoid ships, cars, and trains, nine-deck air-

8. Norman Bel Geddes. Gas Range. 1932. (*From the work of Norman Bel Geddes at the Hoblitzelle Theatre Arts Library, The Humanities Research Center, University of Texas, by permission of the executrix Edith Lutyens Bel Geddes.*)

liners, multi-cellular houses . . . drawings [which] have made the Geddes myth." [9]

Geddes's advanced thinking—which brought forth the first streamlined ocean liner (1927), a turntable landing strip for Manhattan (1928), a rotating restaurant atop a tower (1929), a gigantic flying-wing airliner (1929), streamlined cars, buses and trains (1930–34)—called attention to the new profession; his more ordinary work gained respect for industrial designers, proving their worth and practicality. For the Standard Gas Equipment Corporation he designed the prototype of the modern kitchen range (fig. 8). He sought utmost simplicity, eliminating projections and dirt-catching corners and minimizing cracks and joints. Oven doors acted as shelves when open and closed flush with the front surface. Surface burners were covered with a hinged panel when not in use so that there was no evidence that the enameled cabinet was a stove. Legs were eliminated (along with the need for cleaning underneath), and the resultant space was utilized for pot storage. The ivory-white vitreous enamel and chromed hardware was easy to clean, for "immaculateness was a major consideration in the design." [10]

Geddes "streamlined" production of S.G.E.C.'s entire line of ranges, which had included a hundred models and sizes. By creating twelve modules that could be combined in many ways he effected cost savings. The use of spring clips speeded assembly; and by relieving the enameled parts of structural tension he reduced cracking and flaking during shipment. All were logical, useful innovations that reduced costs, improved the product and made it more attractive to the consumer.

Henry Dreyfuss, also a successful theatrical designer, entered what he called the "unknown and experimental profession" of industrial design in 1929. His early works ranged from perfume bottles to home appliances and office machines. In 1930 he began to modernize the modern cradle telephone and continued to do so as technology provided new and lighter materials and smaller components. Dreyfuss made moderate use of aerodynamics. He did not dwell upon the future, but concentrated instead on the immediate environment of homes, offices, ocean liners and trains. In his biography, *Designing for People* (1955), he used the expression "cleanlining" to describe his approach to redesigning existing products.[11] Dreyfuss never startled; his sense of proportion, texture and finish led, over his long career, to unobtrusive but handsome objects that raised the public's level of taste.

Walter Dorwin Teague achieved prominence in the mid-twenties as an advertising artist and as an authority on typography. By 1927 he began to design products and packaging as well. The following year he began an association with Eastman Kodak (fig. 9) and by 1930 was devoting all his energies to industrial design. Like the French architect Le Corbusier, whose ideas had interested him since 1926, Teague saw analogies between the mathematical proportions of the Parthenon and the functionalism of modern aircraft and automobiles. No project was too small or too large for the Teague firm. *Design This Day* (1940) is Teague's record of a decade of activities and a statement of his philosophy.[12]

9.   Walter Dorwin Teague. Kodak *Bantam Special* Camera. 1936. (*Courtesy the Eastman Kodak Company.*)

Raymond Loewy was trained as an engineer in Paris and served in the Great War. After the Armistice he set out for America and an engineering career. His talent for sketching led to graphics for *Vogue* and *Harper's Bazaar* and window displays for Macy's and Saks Fifth Avenue. Loewy opened his New York industrial design office in 1930 and counted among his clients the Hupmobile Company; Sears, Roebuck and Company, for whom he designed the 1935 and later Coldspot refrigerators; and the Pennsylvania Railroad, whose engines he streamlined. After World War II he began to design Studebaker cars, including the Avanti. *Never Leave Well Enough Alone,* published in 1951, is his resume of experiences as a leading designer. His refined sensibility has graced products large and small.[13]

Richard Buckminster Fuller is a designer-architect-engineer whose fertile mind encompasses the entire range of design problems, from closet storage to the world's population and energy problems. He has long concerned himself with the question of how technology can maximize the benefits derived from an understanding and control of the forces of nature. According to his "Dymaxion" concept, rational action in a rational world demands the most efficient overall performance per units of input in every social and industrial operation.[14] His geodesic domes manifest that philosophy by spanning maximum floor space with minimal structural weight. His early childhood on an island-farm provided experience in building simple tools and machinery and in the construction and operation of small sailing craft.[15] At Milton Academy he acquired a solid theoretical education. After two years at Harvard, he left to become an apprentice machinist. As a Navy seaman during the First World War he became acquainted with aircraft and radio.

Fuller's interest in construction and modern technology resulted in his Dymaxion house of 1927. Had the industry adopted the materials and assembly-line procedures of the airframe companies, his architecture would, he felt, have been lower in cost and light enough to deliver to the site by dirigible. That same year he designed his "4-D Zoomobile," an auto-airplane meant to be capable of lifting off the highways. Subsequent *Dymaxion Cars* utilized aerodynamic principles and aircraft construction techniques.

Like his patents, Fuller's writings are numerous and seminal. *4D Time Lock* outlined his attitudes on the application of modern technology to housing problems.[16] *Nine Chains to the Moon* deals with rational planning and the need for a broad overview of the universe.[17] *Ideas and Integrities, A Spontaneous Autobiographical Disclosure,* is just that and continues his ruminations on demography, world planning and the future.

Otto Kuhler had drawn automobile body designs as a child in Germany. By twenty he was a consultant to body builders in Berlin and Brussels. His mechanical engineering education evolved from formal training in and around his family's steelworks. During the First World War he supervised the construction of a railroad in Belgium. For a short time after the Armistice he studied art in Düsseldorf. In 1923 he arrived in Pittsburgh with his Belgian wife Simonne and with eight dollars in his pockets. With a background in mills and foundries he was able to make accurate and precise (albeit romantic) etchings and paintings of the industrial scene. He supported himself as an artist until 1932 when he became a consultant designer for the American Locomotive Company. These experiences, along with his later careers as a cattle rancher and painter of the southwest, are retold in his autobiography *My Iron Journey* (1967).[18]

Geddes, Dreyfuss, Teague, Loewy, Kuhler and several other designers, including John Vassos, Russel Wright, Peter Mueller-Munk and Egmont Arens, shaped the profession during the thirties, establishing good taste and sound professional practice and improving upon the utility, safety and appearance of products. In the process they acquired an understanding of industrial methods and raised challenges for American technology. Above all they encouraged an interest in the potential of the future and, by spurring sales, aided in the economic recovery.

## TECHNOCRACY

That an economy attuned to scientific developments and quick to convert them to technological advantage should suddenly grind to a halt seemed an impossible nightmare to many in the first years after the Crash. Men were willing but unable to work in a nation rich with resources, and established orthodoxies came under question. The value of an education, the ethic of hard work and perseverance and the wisdom of banking earnings were absolutes that had always been taken for granted. If these myths died, new ones arose quickly. That spending could lead back to prosperity, for example, was a new credo requiring convincing arguments, but it was a time for listening.

The Technocrats held the public's attention for a short time in 1932 and 1933. Howard Scott, leader of the Technocrats and a student of the writings of Thorstein Veblen and Frederick Soddy, engineered an "Energy Survey of North America" with a group of idled architects based at Columbia University.[19] He felt that engineers and scientists could provide leadership superior to that of the politicians. Scott thought America's technical and industrial systems were workable but that our banking and credit systems had interfered with them. He proposed a new price system based on energy units such as ergs and joules. The implementation of such a changeover would have been an enormous task. The public opted instead for the New Deal.

## CONSUMER ENGINEERING

Most agreed that stimulating sales would increase employment and the spiral would begin upward once again. A master planner was needed to orchestrate the many specialists who would partake; in 1932 it appeared he would be called a "consumer engineer." His task was to shape a product to fit the consumer's needs or tastes—and, more broadly, to take any actions that might lead to increased consumption of goods and services. To do this he would find it expedient to "organize and coordinate the creative efforts of artists, designers, inventors, machinists, merchandisers, advertising men, and fashion coordinators" in the work of his associate, the "industrial stylist." [20] As it turned out, the latter became the coordinator and included specialists on his staff or retained them as consultants; the industrial designer became a "consumer engineer."

When Sheldon and Arens published *Consumer Engineering* they reflected a general dissatisfaction with goods and services, quite natural in a time of turmoil. They found fault with housing, transportation, packaging and other areas requiring the designer's attention. Where improvements had been made in the few short years of the design profession, they made note of them, particularly when these had been made possible by new materials and processes. The book urged businessmen to examine their image and their products to see if they were responding to changes in society. They reminded them that the American woman was less isolated and had become more discriminating. "The magazines, the newspapers, the radio, and the movies all told her and showed her what was in style." [21]

Obsolescence was a positive factor in designing and merchandising, a "thrusting force which clears the way for the more desirable product, the more convenient article, the more beautiful object," and the means of freedom from the "shackles of tradition." As examples of unorthodox solutions they cited the propeller-driven *Rail Zeppelin* being tested on German railways, Colonel Seagrave's latest successes in race car designs and Dr. Tietjen's tests of streamlined model vehicles in Westinghouse's wind tunnels.[22] Such new developments, as Sheldon and Arens saw it, made obsolescence inevitable.

Psychology had been used in advertising and marketing, but the new consumer engineers would utilize *behaviorism*, with which advertisers were experimenting. "The net results of all these investigations is a new dynamic psychology which has all the liveliness of suggestion that the outdated metaphysical psychology lacked. It thinks in terms of activities and strivings, of impulses and conflicts, of reflexes and inhibitions; in such terms that the merchandising practitioner can lay hold of them and use them to his active advantage." [23] By 1932 Sheldon and Arens like many others had lost faith in politicians; converting the unemployed into consumers was "a problem in human engineering which political muddling will not solve." [24]

## A NEW HORIZON

While others castigated staid political policies that failed to cope with economic crises, or cited the failure of industries to create demands for products as the cause of the persistence of the Depression, Norman Bel Geddes took a more positive approach. In *Horizons* he acknowledged the pressure, complexity and discordance of the contemporary scene, but he sensed that apathy was the least of the problems. "Never before," he wrote, "in an economic crisis, has there been such an aroused consciousness on the part of the community at large and within industry itself. Complacency has vanished. A new horizon appears. A horizon that will inspire the next phase in the evolution of the age." [25]

*Horizons* was perhaps the first comprehensive exposition of the potential of design applied to transportation, products and housing. Geddes implied that reasoned design could effect social organization to provide work, wealth and leisure, could be applied to industry to improve working conditions, could make objects of daily use economical, durable and convenient—and that, applied to the arts, design would inspire the new era.[26] He referred to recent (and often experimental) advances in high-speed railroads, race cars and aircraft and sketched a vision of the future when travel would be convenient, luxurious and economical. In each case aerodynamic streamlining would reduce the energy expended; designs of his own—airliners, autos, buses and trains—provided a preview of that future. Products would take advantage of easily maintainable materials and finishes and save drudgery. Here, Geddes was able to illustrate *Horizons* with designs he had created for Toledo Scales, Simmons Furniture, Standard Gas Equipment and other clients.

Geddes's architectural concepts ranged from the spectacular to the practical. For the Century of Progress Exposition held in Chicago in 1933 he proposed an aquarium restaurant (fig. 10) under a waterfall and an aerial restaurant (fig. 11) which would revolve slowly atop a 278-foot stem

10.   Norman Bel Geddes. *Aquarium Restaurant*. 1932. (*From the work of Norman Bel Geddes at the Hoblitzelle Theatre Arts Library, The Humanities Research Center, University of Texas, by permission of the executrix Edith Lutyens Bel Geddes.*)

and provide seating for twelve hundred diners in a three-level facility. The economic situation prohibited construction, but a structure similar to the aerial restaurant was developed for the 1962 World's Fair in Seattle. Domestic architecture also interested Geddes and in this case "streamlining" consisted of providing an efficient and manageable house.

*Horizons* was a seminal work that did more than popularize streamlining and offer an imaginative glimpse of the future. Geddes relied upon the research of others; the technical aspects of aerodynamics were widely known and were being applied to vehicles. His contribution was the promotion of good design principles and procedures and their application to all areas of activity. He wrote about *essential forms* evolved from their conditions of use, a variant on Sullivan's form-follows-function credo. These essential forms have an inherent beauty, Geddes felt, a logic that bespeaks of their functions. No additions are necessary, but the artist who knows how to create beauty with a minimum of means must collaborate with the engineer to assure that the form is as visually pleasing as it is logical. The final product ought to have the approval of both engineer and artist.[27] Geddes was well aware of the excesses of the Victorian period when engineers, patternmakers and machinists "beautified" objects by adding ornamentation, and he had learned the virtue of simplicity preached by the Bauhaus masters.

At the beginning of a new profession in America, Geddes set forth sound design procedures. Industrial designers would:

1. Determine the specific design objectives: the intended function of a product, the way it is made, sold and serviced.
2. Visit the client's factory and determine the capacity and limitations of the machines and the workers. Perform a cost analysis of the manufacturing, distribution and promotion of the product.

3. Research the competition, surveying the consumers' attitudes, and test the competitive product to determine its good and bad points.
4. Consider the opinions of salesmen, engineers, advertisers and other specialists.[28]

By his attention to transportation, public buildings, domestic architecture and household convenience, Geddes alerted manufacturers to po-

11. Norman Bel Geddes. *Revolving Restaurant.* 1932. (*From the work of Norman Bel Geddes at the Hoblitzelle Theatre Arts Library, The Humanities Research Center, University of Texas, by permission of the executrix Edith Lutyens Bel Geddes.*)

12.  Claude Dornier. The *DO-X*. 1929. (*Courtesy Macdonald and Jane's Publishers, London.*)

tential new markets while helping to create a desire for new goods among laymen. Broad design services became a hallmark of industrial designers. By the end of the decade Geddes had begun to take a macro-view of design, concerning himself with entire systems as well as individual components. For the Futurama exhibit of 1939 (see Chapter 8) he envisioned a total urban-rural environment interconnected by superhighways.

Norman Bel Geddes was embarrassed to be identified as "the father of streamlining." [29] Nevertheless he popularized a new aesthetic of dynamic functional forms, of smooth organic shells consistent with known aerodynamic principles. His "teardrop" became more than an ideal form, it became a symbol of progress that would be wrought from the application of science and aesthetics to design problems.

## BY AIR TOMORROW

Undoubtedly, the modern airplane was the most pervasive influence in the shift from angular, geometric Art Deco forms to the new smooth organic forms of the Streamlined Decade. Even in its earlier form (boxy open frames with struts and guy wires), the airplane had been a symbol of a new level of achievement, man's long-sought freedom from gravity. Structural improvements led to the elimination of drag-inducing guy wires, and in the later 1920s aircraft had evolved to simpler forms. Lindbergh's solo flight over the Atlantic in 1927 added a new chapter in the story of heroic adventures in the air, and the *Spirit of St. Louis* began appearing in murals in new skyscrapers, hotel lobbies and movie palaces.

Until 1929, coast-to-coast air service was not available, though one could make the trip in forty-eight hours with a combination of daytime flights and night trains.[30] Cooperative ventures between railroads and

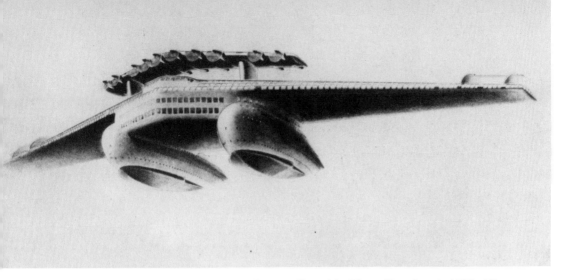

13.  Norman Bel Geddes with Dr. Otto Koller. *Air Liner Number 4.* 1929. (*From the work of Norman Bel Geddes at the Hoblitzelle Theatre Arts Library, The Humanities Research Center, University of Texas, by permission of the executrix Edith Lutyens Bel Geddes.*)

airlines were abandoned as the range of aircraft improved and air terminals added lights to their landing strips. The airplane quickly gained the advantage of high speed, threatening the railroads and later the steamship lines, for amphibian planes that could carry a light load of passengers were in service by 1928.

What an early air traveler gained in time he lost in conveniences. Needed were aircraft that could provide comfortable dining and sleeping arrangements. Claude Dornier, at one time an assistant to Count von Zeppelin, designed a prototype of such a craft at his plant in Friedrichshafen. When the *DO-X* (fig. 12) first flew in July 1929, it was the largest airplane in the world. Its hull closely resembled that of a ship, complete with portholes and a "bridge." With a wingspread of 157 feet and a length of 131 feet, the 48-ton "flying boat" was designed to carry 150 passengers and a crew of ten. It exceeded that; on its maiden flight nine stowaways concealed themselves among the three decks.[31]

Norman Bel Geddes was reported to have challenged his staff to dream up the best way of getting "a thousand luxury lovers from New York to Paris fast. Forget the limitations." [32] In *Horizons* he acknowledged Dornier's accomplishments and presented a scaled-up, more luxurious version of the *DO-X.* He had begun designing *Air Liner Number 4* (fig. 13) in 1929 in collaboration with Dr. Otto Koller, designer of over two hundred airplanes and former chief engineer of Germany's military aircraft. They conceived of a tail-less flying wing with a span of 528 feet that would provide its 451 passengers and 115 crew members "recreations and diversions" such as were found on ocean liners. Geddes insisted it was not a mad or foolish idea, nor was it big for the sake of being big.[33]

In light of today's jumbo jets, *Air Liner Number 4* was not unreasonable in its seating capacity but it was slow by comparison, being

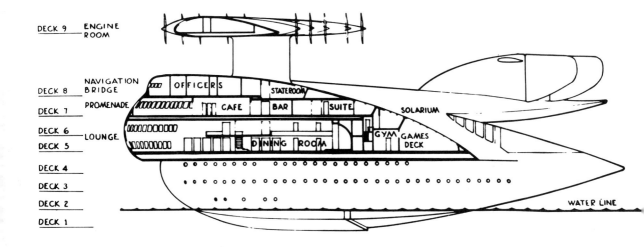

DECK 9 — ENGINE ROOM

DECK 8 — NAVIGATION BRIDGE

DECK 7 — PROMENADE

DECK 6 — LOUNGE

DECK 5

DECK 4

DECK 3

DECK 2

DECK 1

OFFICERS

STATEROOM

CAFE   BAR   SUITE

SOLARIUM

DINING ROOM

GYM   GAMES DECK

WATER LINE

14. Norman Bel Geddes. *Air Liner Number 4. 1929. (From the work of Norman Bel Geddes at the Hoblitzelle Theatre Arts Library, The Humanities Research Center, University of Texas, by permission of the executrix Edith Lutyens Bel Geddes.)*

15. Norman Bel Geddes. *Air Liner Number 4. 1929. (From the work of Norman Bel Geddes at the Hoblitzelle Theatre Arts Library, The Humanities Research Center, University of Texas, by permission of the executrix Edith Lutyens Bel Geddes.)*

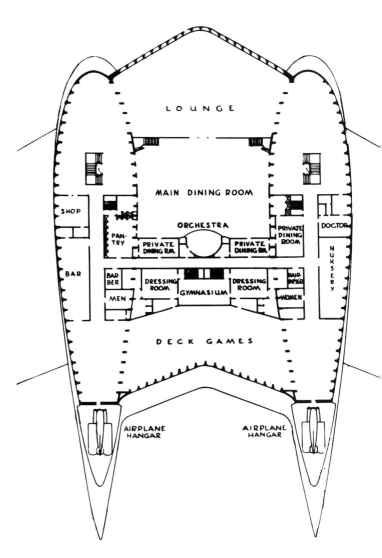

LOUNGE

MAIN DINING ROOM

ORCHESTRA

SHOP

PANTRY

PRIVATE DINING RM.

PRIVATE DINING RM.

PRIVATE DINING ROOM

DOCTOR

NURSERY

BAR

BARBER

MEN

DRESSING ROOM

GYMNASIUM

DRESSING ROOM

HAIR DRSR.

WOMEN

DECK GAMES

AIRPLANE HANGAR

AIRPLANE HANGAR

dependent upon piston engines. By Geddes's best estimates it would take forty-two hours for this airliner to make the Chicago to London run with a cruising speed of 100 mph. From his viewpoint it was fast, for it would make possible three transatlantic crossings each week; ocean liners could manage but one. Moreover, it could be built at a fraction of the cost of a luxury ship and fares equivalent to first-class steamship passage (about $300 in 1932) would be justified by the accommodations and service.

The main wing would rest upon two huge teardrop-shaped pontoons (fig. 14). A secondary wing and its twenty engines would lift the huge amphibian. Six spare engines within the power wing could be rolled into position in the event of an in-flight failure. The remaining decks were connected by elevators. Deck 7 was to be promenade deck; passengers could stroll along the inside of the main wing's leading edge with its large shatterproof windows or sit in one of the 150 deck chairs. On this same deck would be staterooms, baths and suites, the latter having living rooms, bedrooms and enclosed verandas. All rooms would have telephones and running water.

On a lower deck (fig. 15) passengers could avail themselves of the lounge, foyers, main or private dining room, barber or beauty salon, gymnasium, nursery, bar or sickbay. Among the crew were to be listed a nursemaid, a physician, a masseuse and a masseur, wine stewards and a librar-

16. The Northrup Company. The *YB–49*. Mid 1940s. (*Official U.S. Air Force photo.*)

ian. Clearly, Geddes intended to combine the conveniences of the ocean liners with the experience of Zeppelin travel.

The two pontoons served as crew quarters and storage space for six life boats and two small airplanes which could be launched to the rear during flight. (The U.S. Navy was testing the feasibility of using dirigibles to launch small planes the same year *Horizons* was published.) *Air Liner Number 4* was projected for 1940 and seems to have been within the realm of technical possibility. Experimental "flying wings" were built by the Northrup Company in the mid-forties (fig. 16). An examination of the Pan-American Airlines "Clipper" ships will reveal that several features of *Air Liner Number 4* were put into practice, though not on such a grand scale. Geddes apparently did not forecast jet engines that made large aircraft possible and which shortened long flights to such an extent that diversions like the tennis courts, shuffleboard courts and a seven-piece orchestra would be unnecessary. Nor could he possibly anticipate our preference for electronic and cinematic diversions and our willingness to sacrifice personal space for faster and more economical travel.

## THE FLYING BOATS

Aviation progress has centered upon land-based planes, but those craft incorporating both aerodynamic and hydrodynamic principles—the "flying boats"—played a significant role in the history of transoceanic flight. Pan-American Airlines, founded in 1927, began its 90-mile Key West to Havana mail route with a borrowed *Fairchild FC–2* floatplane.[34] After passenger service was added, and then extended to Miami and Nassau, the decision was made to encircle the Caribbean with land and sea facilities. With Colonel Lindberg's expertise Pan-Am opted for a majority of flying boats and found the light-passenger *Sikorsky S–38* amphibian best suited to its needs. It was cheaper and quicker to set up waterborne operations than to build landing strips like those on the Texas-Mexico-Central American route. Service around the entire Caribbean became available in 1930.

Flying down to Rio became a reality for Pan-Am passengers that same year when the airline inherited the New York, Rio and Buenos Aires Line as a subsidiary along with a fleet of fourteen Consolidated *Commodore* flying boats, each accommodating twenty-two passengers.[35] Service along the west coast of South America using landplanes had begun the previous year. At this time close cooperation with Igor Sikorsky, the Russian-born builder of the first multimotored airplane (1913), produced the

17.   Igor Sikorsky. The *Southern Clipper*, Sikorsky *S–40*. 1931. (*Pan American World Airways Photo*.)

series of "Clipper" ships that provided comfortable passage around the Caribbean and across the Pacific.

The Sikorsky *S–40* (fig. 17) was the largest airliner built in America up to that time; the first, the *American Clipper*, was christened by Mrs. Herbert Hoover in 1931.[36] The rear cabin of a sister ship, the *Southern Clipper* (fig. 18), entered through a roof hatch, was equipped with marine gear and furnished comfortably in a yacht-club Deco fashion. In the forward cabins, attired in baggy gentility (fig. 19), passengers were served by stewards in nautical dress. These first clippers carried forty passengers and a crew of six down the east coast of South America with Rio as the fifteenth stop from Miami, and Buenos Aires the twenty-second.

Although the *S–42* (fig. 20) carried only thirty-two passengers, it had three times the range of its predecessors, covering 750 miles at 140 mph with an ample baggage and freight load.[37] Ships like the *Bermuda Clipper* achieved a new high in luxury (fig. 21) and performance. They saw service first in Latin America in 1934 but had been developed for the 2,400-mile hop from San Francisco to Hawaii. The Martin *M.130* (fig. 22) exceeded the specification for that task and continued on to the islands of Midway, Wake and Guam and landed finally at Manila, six days out of

18.   Rear cabin of the *Southern Clipper*. (*Pan American World Airways Photo.*)

19.   Forward cabin of the *Southern Clipper*. (*Pan American World Airways Photo.*)

20. Igor Sikorsky. The Sikorsky *S–42. Ca.* 1934. (*Pan American World Airways Photo.*)

San Francisco.[38] Passenger service began in 1936 and extended the next year to Hong Kong aboard the *China Clipper*.

At the end of the decade, a flying boat, far short of Norman Bel Geddes's expectations but far in advance of its competition, began service over both oceans. The Boeing *B–314* was the finest civil passenger flying boat built (figs. 23, 24), designed to carry seventy passengers on short trips and thirty between San Francisco and Hawaii. Like the Geddes *Air Liner Number 4*, engines could be serviced in flight (though not replaced) from the big nacelles behind each motor, each connected by telephone to the bridge. Behind the bridge on the flight deck were the navigation and engineering officers' station, the Captain's office, a large hold, the crew's sleeping quarters and a baggage compartment. On the main deck below were five main passenger cabins, accommodating in all fifty daytime or thirty nighttime passengers, one four-passenger compartment and at the stern a completely furnished private "Bridal Suite." [39]

The dining-lounge compartment was designed to serve fifteen passengers at a time. Gone now were the nautical trappings of earlier Pan-Am *Clippers*. The smart set upgraded their fashions to meet the functional but modern decor (fig. 25) and were provided with separate men's and women's dressing rooms and lavatories. The *B–314s* flew over northern and southern Pacific routes and in 1939, as the *Yankee Clipper*, initiated runs from New York to Shediac, New Brunswick, Botwood, Newfoundland and Foynes, Ireland, and a southern route from New York to the Azores and Lisbon.[40] On the day before the attack upon Pearl Harbor another route was opened at the request of President Roosevelt. This run, from Miami to Leopoldville, formed the basis of a ferry service that later supported the Allied drive in North Africa. Several *B–314s* were converted to

21. Aboard the *Bermuda Clipper*. (*Pan American World Airways Photo.*)

22. The Glen Martin Company. The *China Clipper*, Martin *M. 130*. (*Pan American World Airways Photo.*)

23.   Boeing Aircraft. The Boeing *B–314*. In service by 1939. (*Pan American World Airways Photo.*)

24.   The *B–314* taking off. (*Pan American World Airways Photo.*)

wartime use and the lighter PBY "Catalinas" were developed for sea rescue and reconnaissance. Flying boats carried civilian passengers briefly after the war, but faster landplanes like the *DC–4* brought an end to this very distinctive form of travel.

## THE FULLY STREAMLINED AIRPLANE

The boxy shape of aircraft gradually experienced a metamorphosis into an organic form; by 1933 it had become fully streamlined. As early as 1921 Boeing's military pursuit planes had featured a projectile-like propeller hub that blended with a streamlined engine cowling, giving the front a smooth, continuous profile.[41] Racing planes began to incorporate low-resistance forms as fully as possible. The 1930 Curtiss-Hawk featured teardrop wheel pants and "a beautifully streamlined body." Captain Frank Hawks had hit upon "the secret of aviation speed." [42] Similar forms were developing in race cars, connecting science with daredevilry and suggesting forms that would later be exploited by Detroit automakers.

In 1932 Jack Frye, guiding light of Transcontinental and Western

25.   Dining area of a *B–314*. (*Pan American World Airways Photo.*)

26.  Douglas Aircraft. Interior of the Douglas *DC–2*. 1934. (*Courtesy McDonnell Douglas Corporation.*)

Air, asked his directors, engineers, pilots and mechanics to list the qualities of an ideal airplane. From their suggestions he compiled specifications and submitted them to manufacturers. Donald Douglas assigned each of his specialists to the task, and soon a design was on the Douglas Aircraft drawing boards. It adapted some features of a modified delta wing designed by Jack Northrup, but the engines—the Wright A-Cylinder, 750 hp. "Cyclones"—were a new and radical development.[43] A prototype —the *DC–1* (Douglas Commercial One)—was flown in July 1933 and released to TWA for testing. Boeing introduced its twin-engined *247* that year. Both planes had the now familiar form of multiengine transport planes, with hemispherical noses, tapering cylindrical fuselages, and sweptback wings and stabilizers. The logic of aerodynamics was now clearly stated in a form that revealed its function while summing up and symbolizing the ideas of flight, lift and low resistance.

27.   Douglas Aircraft. The Douglas *DC–3*. 1935. (*Courtesy American Airlines.*)

Only a single *DC–1* was built. TWA requested modifications and the *DC–2s* were tested in 1934. The fourteen to eighteen seats were arranged in single rows (fig. 26). Because the plane wasn't wide enough to accommodate berths, a final redesign was ordered. The larger version was intended as a luxury sleeper for American Airlines with seven upper and seven lower berths and a private cabin forward. Engineers discovered that instead of berths, three rows of seven seats could be fitted into the fuselage. As a twenty-one passenger liner with increased range the *DC–3* (fig. 27) went into service in 1936 on American's nonstop New York-to-Chicago run.[44] The appearance of these first fully streamlined passenger planes made the public aware of and interested in aerodynamic designs. The rounded contours and unified form became a symbol of technological progress that influenced the design of trains, automobiles and other objects.

The *DC–3* cut coast-to-coast travel to fifteen hours with a cruising speed of 165 to 180 miles per hour, thereby attracting celebrities who shuttled from Broadway to Hollywood and back, adding a note of glamour to transcontinental flights. The new plane freed the airlines from complete dependence upon government mail contracts, for it was the first airplane to turn a profit on passenger fares alone.[45] Indeed, its economy was such as to allow upper-middle class families to charter flights for special events (fig. 28), initiating a new life-style. The plane became a standard on major American airlines and many foreign ones; thousands are still in service.

When the French architect Le Corbusier wrote *Towards a New Architecture* in 1923, he included sections on ocean liners, airplanes and automobiles—all examples, he felt, of designs that respond to needs. All were object-lessons for architects, and the lesson of the airplane "lies in the logic which governed the statement of the problem and its realization." [46] He returned to the subject with another book, *Aircraft* (1935), in which he described the airplane as a "symbol of the New Age . . . [an] advance guard of the conquering armies of the New Age, the airplane

28. A family outing on an American Airlines *DC-3*. 1939. (*Author's Collection.*)

arouses our energies and our faith." The public, unfortunately, was un-interested in the struggle to improve aircraft design. Only the sensational news of Lindbergh's transatlantic crossing excited them:

> *The masses do not want facts, reasoning, calculation, theorems . . . they must have sensational demonstrations that are symbolic as they conceive symbolism. . . . They must have a spectacle.*[47]

But Le Corbusier was not discouraged, for the airplane had given us a clear vision; our minds could then make clear decisions.

Seldon Cheney agreed with Le Corbusier, writing in 1936 that "the airplane, with its symbol the streamline, is the most conspicuous object of the new age." [48] Norman Bel Geddes considered "the stirring beauty of airplanes" an emotional response to their functional forms.[49] The *DC–3* was particularly moving to Walter Dorwin Teague. Everywhere in the plane he found a recurring contour line consisting of a short parabolic arc combined with a graceful sweeping curve. The nose thrust forward, its profile relaxing past the cockpit and easing to the rear. The rudder had a similar profile, rising slowly, then arching over suddenly and dropping to the rear tip of the fuselage. There was, Teague wrote, no more exciting form in modern design.[50]

In 1933 the fully streamlined airplane became the norm, and all aircraft thereafter would assume smooth rounded surfaces and graceful organic curves free of protrusions. Flight had taken on a distinctively modern new form in an even more effective symbol. Small wonder that the new industrial designers admired these forms; they were justified in na-ture and now in manned flight. For some designers it was time to apply aerodynamic principles to other vehicles. For others, the new planes exem-plified an aesthetic of clean organic forms that could be applied to products of all types.

## IDEAL FORMS

When he began redesigning the American automobile, Norman Bel Geddes modeled the superstructure "as near the drop form as it is prac-ticable," predicting that an enlightened manufacturer would soon follow suit and use this same "ultimate form of the future motor car." [51] Walter Dorwin Teague said of the automobiles of 1940 that even the best designs were still far from "that sleek tear-drop shape we believe will be their ultimate form." [52] Henry Dreyfuss wrote that during the thirties the teardrop had been held up as an *ideal form*. The terms *teardrop, drop form* and *stream form* were being used interchangeably and all referred to what Cayley called his "true solid of least resistance." That a falling drop of water assumed other forms was immaterial; it looked that way just before it fell from a tap, and artists had long been using the convention to depict raindrops. A mythic form became in the Streamlined Decade both a symbol and a platonic ideal, approximations of which seemed to hold promise in reducing waste and increasing speed.

For his radical aircraft design of 1927, Richard Buckminster Fuller fitted out a teardrop form with a rudder, stabilizers and inflatable wings (fig. 29). Since 1917 he had been considering the utility of a personal transport unit which would make it possible to locate the family dwelling in areas remote from highways. His "4D twin, angularly-orientable, individually throttleable, jet-stilt, controlled-plummeting transport" or Zoomobile would be lifted and directed by jet thrusts, three liquid-air turbines beneath the vehicle.[53] Fuller designed the vehicle as an automobile that could metamorphose into an airplane and spring from the highway into

29. Richard Buckminster Fuller. The *4D Zoomobile*. 1927. (*R. Buckminster Fuller.*)

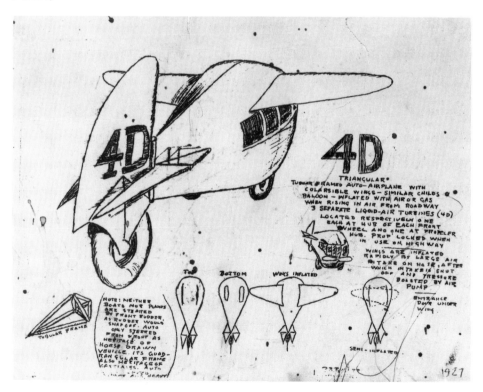

the sky. In flight, a propeller at the bow end would provide forward movement and the wings would be kept rigid by an air pump. In its automotive mode, the Zoomobile's wings would be deflated and its propeller locked in position. In appearance the vehicle resembled small amphibious aircraft of the forties; in principle it anticipated some features of NASA's moon-landing craft, also steerable by jet thrusts.

Fuller ventured into projects armed with an understanding of structures, energy systems and the ability to anticipate problems and evolve unique solutions. The designers with art backgrounds tended to base their projections on recent successes. But like Fuller, they recognized the value of what was being accepted as an ideal form, and the "teardrop" was endorsed by artist and engineer alike.

# IV.
# THE DYNAMICS OF
# TWO FLUIDS:
# THE
# STREAMLINED SHIP

*Observe a ship at sea! Mark the majestic form of her hull as she*
*rushes through the water, observe the graceful blend of her body,*
*the gentle transition from round to flat, the grasp of her keel, the*
*leap of her bows. . . . Here is the result of the study of man upon the*
*great deep, where Nature spoke of the laws of building . . . in wind*
*and waves, and he bent all his mind to hear and to obey.*[1]

Thus did Horatio Greenough, the American neoclassic sculptor, in 1843
extoll the designers of the great American clipper ships. By the empirical
method of observation and testing they had made their hulls and sails con-
form to the fluid environments of air and water. The new ships, designed
with long, gently graduated bows, rode heavy seas without taking in water
over their sides. Their performance was quite in contrast to that of the
English ship with its short heavy bow and massive bowsprit—a spar extending from the upper end of the bow, described by one disgruntled
British captain as "a bow-plunging, speed-stopping, money-spending, and
absurd acquiescence in old-fashioned prejudices about appearances. . . ."[2]
In the spirit of economy and efficiency, Yankee shipbuilders had wisely

obeyed what Ralph Waldo Emerson called "the law of fluids that prescribes the shape of the boat,—keel, rudder, and bows,—and, in the finer fluid above, the form and tackle of the sails." [3] Emerson agreed with Aristotle's definition of the art of shipbuilding as "all of the ship but the wood"; art being, universally, the spirit creative, the reason of the thing without the matter.[4]

Emerson's viewpoint was Transcendentalist: to make anything useful or beautiful the individual must submit to the "universal soul," the "alone creator." Nature is the omnipotent agent and representative of the universal mind and designers must heed her wishes, for "the first and last lesson of the useful arts is, that nature tyrannizes over our works. They must be conformed to her law, or they will be ground to powder by her omnipresent activity." [5] In one passage, Emerson interrelated beauty, adaptation and teleological functionalism:

> *Arising out of eternal reason, one and perfect, whatever is beautiful rests on the foundation of the necessary. Nothing is arbitrary, nothing is insulated in beauty. It depends forever on the necessary and the useful. The plumage of the bird, the mimic plumage of the insect, has a reason for its rich colors in the constitution of the animal. Fitness is so inseparable an accompaniment of beauty, that it has been taken for it. The most perfect form to answer an end, is so far beautiful.[6]*

The American naval architect John Willis Griffiths was concerned about both the performance and appearance of ships. In 1850 he wrote *A Treatise on Marine and Naval Architecture or Theory and Practice Blended in Shipbuilding* in which he expressed the need to make a vessel *look* as though it would move without the application of power.[7]

In the twentieth century Le Corbusier was among the first to cite the ocean liner as a model to architects stifled by the Beaux Arts tradition of applied historical ornament.[8] He disparaged talk of regenerating French decorative arts.[9] More important was the new spirit aroused by the machine.[10] This new spirit was exemplified by "these formidable affairs that steamships are." He described ocean liners like the *Aquitania*, the *Lamoricière* and the *France* as "an architecture pure, neat, clear, clean and healthy." [11] These ships were designs governed by economy and conditioned by physical necessities (Emerson's "law of fluids") and they obeyed the same evolutionary laws as natural forms. Modern ocean liners manifested the virtues of discipline, harmony and a calm, vital beauty.[12] Le Corbusier edited his illustrations to include only long shots of the liners, views of the sparse, freshly scrubbed promenade decks (with stray ropes and deck chairs neatly stowed away) and a deserted solarium. A view below decks would have foiled the purist illusion his photo-essay created. The *Aquitania* (1914) has been described as a sea-going museum because of its variety of historical decoration.[13] It featured a Carolean smoking room, a Palladian lounge and luxurious suites named for great painters and decorated with reproductions of each Master's most famous works.[14] The designer, Arthur Davis, felt compelled to provide the passengers with floating hotels, for they were not sailors, pirates or yachtsmen but simply travelers seeking comfort.[15]

Norman Bel Geddes paid homage in *Horizons* to the great clippers, four-masted schooners and ocean liners that have aroused admiration and aesthetic satisfaction. Modern ships have been representative, in their functionalism, of modern architecture, for "the ship has had the same logical development at the hands of men of the sea as the airplane has had at the hands of men of the air." [16] But Geddes deplored the commercial minds who were redecorating ocean liners in period styles reminiscent of baronial halls. Equally distasteful was the pseudo-modern decor of the latest French and German liners.[17] A liner, Geddes felt, ought to develop within the organic terms of ship architecture, not land architecture. Modern liners ought to be built along "advanced" lines, by which he meant aerodynamic principles. In an article published in 1934, Geddes presented the fundamentals of streamlining in terms and with diagrams the layman could grasp.[18] For each mode of transport he delineated the fundamental problems of wind resistance. His description of the turbulence around a conventional ship approached a poetic metaphor:

> It climbs on deck and swirls around ventilators, towing bitts, hoists, life-boats, davits and life-belt boxes. It eddies around the wings of the bridge, the masts and the funnels. Were it possible to photograph the path of air passing over a ship it would surely resemble a tangled skein of yarn.[19]

The logical solution was to enclose the ship in a shell of steel and glass, free of any protuberances or pockets that might induce drag either above or below the water line. Not only would the ship be more efficient, it probably would have an increased carrying capacity. A streamlined ship would tend to be tubular in cross-section, allowing *monocoque* construction which would reduce the ship's dead weight and increase its strength.[20]

Geddes had designed the first such ship in 1927.[21] In *Horizons* he presented plans and models of a more recent version, one more nearly adaptable to the "ideal" teardrop than his other transport designs (fig.

30. Norman Bel Geddes. *Ocean Liner.* 1932. (*From the work of Norman Bel Geddes at the Hoblitzelle Theatre Arts Library, The Humanities Research Center, University of Texas, by permission of the executrix Edith Lutyens Bel Geddes.*)

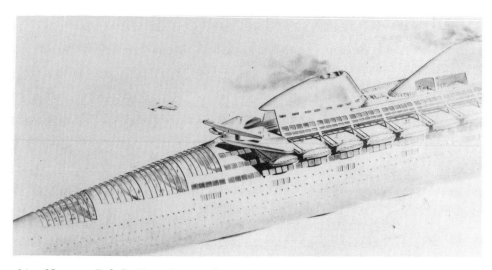

31. Norman Bel Geddes. *Ocean Liner* with the lifeboats extended and the flight deck open. (*From the work of Norman Bel Geddes at the Hoblitzelle Theatre Arts Library, The Humanities Research Center, University of Texas, by permission of the executrix Edith Lutyens Bel Geddes.*)

30). The model shows the influence of modern biomorphic sculpture. The only protrusions on his *Ocean Liner* were the navigator's bridge, which was given the shape of an aircraft wing to lessen its drag, and the smokestacks, oval on the inside but "dissolving" into the mass of the ship with gentle transitional curves.[22] This extensive streamlined cowling represented no waste space, for behind the forward stack the shell covered a café with space for a dance floor and a bar. Under the streamlined foil of the rear stack Geddes provided a machine shop and a hangar for two trimotored seaplanes (fig. 31).[23] Upon the sounding of an alarm, the lifeboats, normally contained within the shell, would slide out horizontally. Each of the twenty-six lifeboats was an enclosed streamlined pod containing a radio and two weeks' rations. Portions of the main shell could be opened during good weather; air conditioning kept the interior of the closed shell comfortable. The glassed areas allowed the sun to shine upon the tennis courts and sand beach. Plan views suggest there was but one class of accommodations, a development that was already under way and which has been identified as an American idea.[24]

A comparison with ships actually built in the 1930s suggests Geddes's *Ocean Liner* would have been competitive in tonnage but longer and slimmer. His calculations estimated a displacement of 70,000 tons, a 110-foot beam, an overall height of 120 feet, and a length of 1,808 feet. The *Queen Mary,* launched in 1934, had a gross tonnage of 81,237, a 118-foot beam, an overall height of 184 feet and was 1,019 feet, 6 inches long.[25] Geddes thought his *Ocean Liner* would cut about twenty-two hours from the New York to Plymouth passage, averaging five and three-quarter knots faster than the *Europa.*[26]

No ship was to appear with the radical and extensive application of streamlining that Geddes envisioned. The *Europa* and her sister ship, the *Bremen,* incorporated in their hulls a form resembling the front of a teardrop. At the front of their keels, well below the waterline, was a bulging extension that reduced the bow waves and the eddy currents along the ships' sides.[27] Above the waterline, however, the ships were closer in spirit to the static functionalism of the Bauhaus than the dynamic functionalism of American streamlined design. The *Bremen's* stacks were short and had an egg-shaped cross-section, both features thought to reduce wind resistance (fig. 32). The forward end of the upper decks and bridge were rounded and swept-back, for the same reason.[28] Inside, the flat surface and the square corner dominated. There was a clean but clinical efficiency about her bare and shiny enameled walls that was relieved only by kitsch decorations.[29]

The *Queen Mary* lacked the low, sleek appearance of the *Bremen.*

32. The *Bremen*. 1929. (*Joe Williamson Marine Photo.*)

Much was made, in fact, of her high-rising stacks, which Cunard publicity material pointed out were taller than the Egyptian obelisk in New York's Central Park. Cunard published a drawing to illustrate the cavernous size of the oval stacks; they were wide enough to allow the passage of three locomotives abreast.[30] Graceful curves at the forward end of the boat deck and bridge gave the ship a moderately streamlined appearance as did the shape and forward slant of her three stacks and her masts (fig. 33). In external appearance, performance and technical design, the *Queen Mary* was the epitome of modernity. The interior decor disappointed those who expected traditional elegance. A decision had been made not to cover cabin walls with the usual attractive fabrics because the public was now sensitive about pests, germs and lingering odors; wood veneers were chosen as a more hygienic surface.[31] The salons were a paean to the Art Deco style. Anna Zinkeisen covered a dance salon wall with gallant young centaurs pursuing a lithe, naked nymph and her fauns. The central shopping concourse resembled the Streamlined Moderne, with sweeping curves, indirect lighting and chromed horizontal bands. The rich warm tones in the glossy veneers and deep-pile carpeting softened the severe geometry. The forward cocktail lounge was all aglitter with chrome bands and cylindrical bar stools and urns.[32]

As one of his first assignments for the Pennsylvania Railroad, Raymond Loewy redesigned a ferryboat. The PRR had its own "navy" consisting at one time of 342 ferries, tugs and barges.[33] The Virginia Ferry Corporation, a subsidiary of the railroad, offered service across the Chesapeake Bay from Cape Charles, Maryland to Norfolk, Virginia. In 1933 Loewy redesigned an older VFC ferry and it was rechristened *The Princess Anne* (after the name of the county in Virginia). The new superstructure was sleek and trim, quite unlike her original architecture. At

33. The *Queen Mary*. 1934. (*Joe Williamson Marine Photo.*)

eighteen statute miles per hour, the 260-foot *Princess Anne* was the largest and fastest ship of its kind (fig. 34). It was hailed as "the ferry transport of tomorrow . . . today" and was built "entirely on modern streamlined principles." [34] Its rounded contours were emphasized by the paint patterns. A view of the top deck (fig. 35) shows the organic contours of a whale-like superstructure, an essential and uncluttered sculptural form. Loewy also designed the *Princess Anne*'s saloon deck, "comparable to that of any first class passenger steamer," which included a lunch counter, dining room and dance floor.[35] Like many other new transport designs of the decade, the streamlined exterior signified a modernized interior and up-

34. Raymond Loewy. The *Princess Anne*. Designed in 1933, launched 1936. (*Raymond Loewy/William Snaith, Inc.*)

35. Raymond Loewy on the top deck of the *Princess Anne*. (*Raymond Loewy/William Snaith, Inc.*)

36. Raymond Loewy and George C. Sharp. The *S.S. Panama*. 1936. (*Raymond Loewy/William Snaith, Inc.*)

37.   Raymond Loewy. Main Salon of the *S.S. Panama*. (*Raymond Loewy/William Snaith, Inc.*)


38.   Raymond Loewy. A stateroom on the *S.S. Panama*. (*Raymond Loewy/William Snaith, Inc.*)

39. The *MV Kalakala*. 1935. (*Joe Williamson Marine Photo.*)

graded services. In 1936 Loewy, in collaboration with naval architect George C. Sharp, designed the *S.S. Panama* (fig. 36) and her sister ships, the *S.S. Cristobal* and the *S.S. Ancon*. Loewy was credited with the "interior design and appointments—decoration and streamlined effects." [36] The main salon was decorated in a style then called "contemporary American," featuring stainless steel, aluminum, glass and synthetic materials (fig. 37). The furnishings had long been rounded for safety and made compact for utility. An updated version of the "yachting style," the decor had bright accents, with stainless steel, mirrors and tubular lighting, contrasting with the walls painted in soft shades of coral, blush-beige and apple green (fig. 38). The three Panama Line ships sailed from New York to Haiti and the Canal Zone until pressed into war service, when the *Panama* served as headquarters for General Eisenhower during the Normandy invasion.

Another ferry streamlined during the 1930s was the *Peralta*, operated by the Key System in San Francisco Bay from 1926 to 1933. After a fire destroyed her upper decks, she was purchased by the Puget Sound Navigation Co. and towed to Washington where she was rebuilt and, in 1935, christened the *M.V. Kalakala* (fig. 39). Advertised as the "world's first streamlined ferry," she provided extra service between Seattle and Bremerton.[37]

40.   Otto Kuhler. Proposal for a modern warship. Early 1940s. (*Courtesy Otto Kuhler.*)

Otto Kuhler spent a lifetime designing streamlined locomotives (see Chapter 5), but every so often "just for the hell of it" he would publish a radical design (fig. 40) to stir up complacent minds.[38] Kuhler's streamlined battleship reminds us that vehicles of war must resist flying projectiles, if not wind and wave. Armored tanks are also streamlined to deflect shells as well as to ease their penetration through dense forests.

# V.
# FLIGHT BY RAIL:
# THE STREAMLINED
# TRAIN

Horatio Greenough expressed great admiration for the vernacular forms evolved in his native land by mechanics unconcerned with fashion and uninhibited by tradition. Clipper ships and trotting wagons were light, graceful and well adapted to their tasks. "The law of adaptation," he wrote, "is the fundamental law of nature in all structure." [1] One could trace man-made objects in their evolution:

> *If we compare the form of a newly invented machine with the perfected type of the same instrument, we observe, as we trace it through the phases of improvement, how weight is shaken off where strength is less needed, how functions are made to approach without impeding each other, how straight becomes curved, and the curve is straightened, till the straggling and cumbersome machine becomes the compact, effective, and beautiful machine.* [2]

Along with functional vernacular forms, Greenough recommended that we consult the "rich mine" of natural forms. The variety and beauty in nature was due not to an arbitrary law of proportion nor to an un-

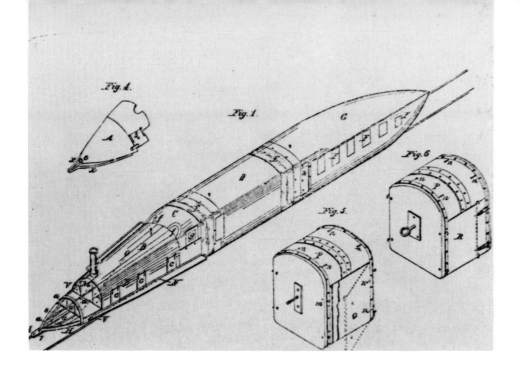

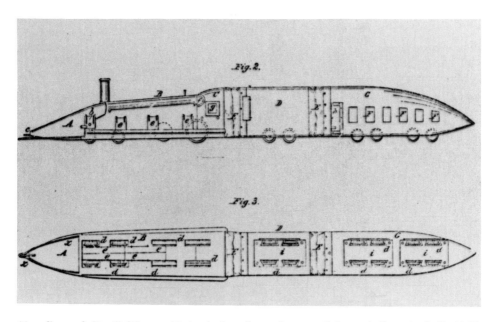

41. Samuel R. Calthrop. Patent drawings for an "air-resisting train." 1865. (*Author's Collection.*)

bending model of form, but to adaptation. Two decades later, a minister in Roxbury, Massachusetts was issued a patent on a machine inspired both by ships and fish. The inventor, Reverend Samuel R. Calthrop, had incorporated a steam engine, tender and passenger car in a single, articulated tapered form (fig. 41), very likely the first streamlined train. The plan view of his "air-resisting train" resembles the outline of a ship's deck, and its profile is similar to an inverted hull. Calthrop's preoccupation with marine forms is evident in his intention to diminish atmospheric friction by

> *... regarding the whole train as an aerial ship and modeling its whole surface in accord with the principles so successfully applied to shipbuilding, modified, however, by the consideration, first, that the railway-train is wholly immersed in the fluid through which it is passing.*[3]

This "aerial ship" was to have both "prow" and "stern," and he sensed the need—six years before the first wind tunnel was built—to taper the rear in order to "overcome the chief part of the resistance arising from the drag of the air behind the rear car in trains as ordinarily constructed."[4] His design would present "a smooth and curving outline to the pressure of the atmospheric fluid, whereby the train may obtain a greater rate of speed with the same consumption of fuel than has heretofore been practicable."[5] Calthrop was familiar with the efficiency of organic forms in penetrating fluids. The front of his engine resembled a "shark's head, which is constructed both for speed when going straight ahead and for rapidity of turning, and therefore has an acute angle at the side as well as in front."[6] In an age when many trains were highly ornamented in Gothic and other styles, Calthrop's understanding of the value of streamlining and his desire to apply it to machinery was remarkable.

At the end of the century, Frederick Upham Adams published his

42. William R. McKeen, Jr. The *McKeen Motor Car*. 1905. (*Union Pacific Railroad Museum Photo.*)

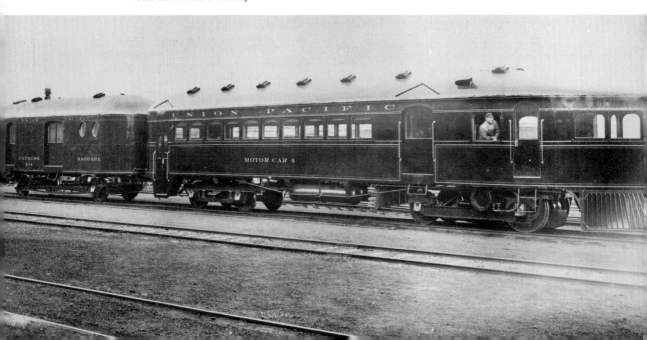

*Atmospheric Resistance and Its Relation to the Speed of Trains* which contained plans for a streamlined train.[7] The Baltimore and Ohio Railroad built and, in 1900, tested a train, the *Windsplitter*, based on Adams's plans. The rear was shaped like a vertical wedge, but conventional locomotives were used in the tests rather than Adams's streamlined engine. Test results were unsatisfactory and the train was dismantled.

The gas-electric railcar was developed to provide low-cost, light branchline service. The internal combustion engine had become practical in the 1880s. In 1890 a railcar was demonstrated by the Patton Motor Car Company that featured an 18-horsepower gasoline engine driving a 12-kilowatt generator that charged a battery.[8] It made little impact on American railroads but it helped inspire French and German designs. In 1908 William R. McKeen, Jr., onetime Superintendent of Motive Power of the Union Pacific Railroad, assumed the presidency of a company that had for four years been building railcars.[9] By 1913 there were 138 McKeen Motor cars in operation; their special characteristic was the pointed knife-like "bow" (fig. 42), which was perhaps more symbolic than functional. The nautical metaphor extended, on some units, to "portholes" as windows. The concern for streamlining was not evident in the interiors, where the vestibules were lined with stained glass, ceilings were decorated with flowers and heat was provided by ornate cast-iron stoves. General Electric built a number of gas-electrics, some of which were given a parabolic shape at each end to reduce wind resistance at high speeds. When the sale of railcars decreased, more attention was given to diesel-electric development, and between 1924 and 1929 a second railcar era flourished and foundations were laid for the eventual dieselization of locomotive rosters.

Otto Kuhler, accustomed to well-manicured European trains, was disappointed when he found outdated equipment and poor service on American railroads during the twenties. He attributed the situation to the strain imposed on them during the First World War when arms and supplies were being shipped to Europe.[10] New competitors had arisen to threaten the financial situation of the railroads: improved highways and lower cost automobiles had made personal mobility democratic, getting people to places inaccessible by rail—and at their own convenience. Though in its infancy, commercial aviation posed an ominous threat with its promise of fast travel. Kuhler thought the railroads needed a new image and decided to create a dramatic symbol by redesigning the steam locomotive. By the light of a kerosene lamp, Kuhler labored for several winter evenings during the recession of 1927.[11] He redesigned a well-known and powerful engine, the New York Central's *J-1* Hudson, in semi- and fully streamlined versions. His paintings were never converted to blue-

43. Raymond Loewy. Propeller-driver rail car. 1932. (*Raymond Loewy/William Snaith, Inc.*)

prints but their publication in 1928 attracted attention and led him to the position of an advertising illustrator and, soon after, an industrial designer with the American Locomotive Company.[12]

In their book *Consumer Engineering*, Sheldon and Arens bemoaned the railroads' "public be damned" attitude and warned that unless speed, economy, comfort and beauty became features of rail travel, passenger service would become obsolete.[13] They recommended the talents of an artist/engineer such as Leonardo da Vinci, in whose mind the practical and the beautiful were wedded. Solutions were in the offing. Dr. Oscar Tietjens was experimenting with streamlined models of autos and trains in the wind tunnels at Westinghouse Electric (another publication suggested Tietjen's reports indicated that "the dawn of a new day in locomotive and coach construction is about to break").[14] Sheldon and Arens also cited Colonel Seagrave's success with streamlined racing cars and

44. Norman Bel Geddes. *Locomotive Number 1*. 1931. (*From the work of Norman Bel Geddes at the Hoblitzelle Theatre Arts Library, The Humanities Research Center, University of Texas, by permission of the executrix Edith Lutyens Bel Geddes.*)

1932

reported on a new experimental German "air-rail passenger car." Franz Kruckenberg and Curt Stedefeld had designed a forty-passenger *Rail Zeppelin* pushed by a four-bladed propeller. The 400-horsepower engine had accelerated it to sixty miles per hour in sixty seconds with a top speed of over 100 miles per hour.[15] Lewis Mumford called the railcar an "experimental and possibly romantic attempt to adapt to surface transportation the advantages of airplane and dirigible."[16] Raymond Loewy designed a lightweight propeller-driven railcar for the Pennsylvania Railroad which was never produced (fig. 43).

Norman Bel Geddes attributed the performance of the *Rail Zeppelin* to its streamlining, its light weight and low center of gravity, factors he thought more significant than its aircraft propeller.[17] He saw the potential for a multiunit train and designed one in 1931, recognizing that the ratio of overall length to width and height of a ten-car train was far

45.  Norman Bel Geddes. *Rear Lounge Car Number 4.* 1931. (*From the work of Norman Bel Geddes at the Hoblitzelle Theatre Arts Library, The Humanities Research Center, University of Texas, by permission of the executrix Edith Lutyens Bel Geddes.*)

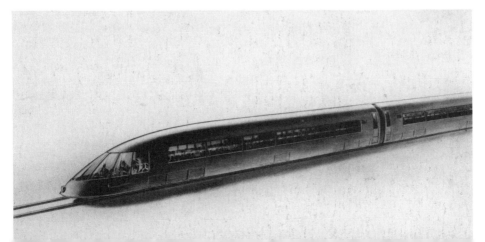

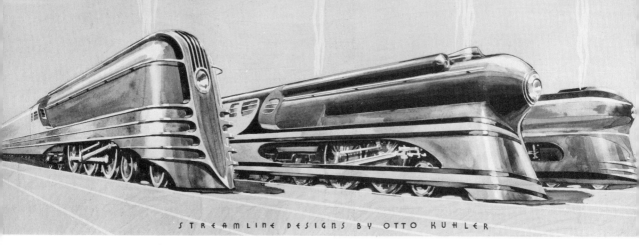

STREAMLINE DESIGNS BY OTTO KUHLER

46. Otto Kuhler. Proposal drawings for streamlined steam engines. 1933. (*Courtesy Otto Kuhler.*)

from that ultimate form, the teardrop. Nevertheless he incorporated streamlining wherever possible. Over a conventional steam engine and tender he sketched a smooth streamform of steel and glass, placing the cab in front for better visibility (fig. 44). All points requiring frequent oiling or inspection were to be accessible by rolling metal shutters which, when closed, conformed to the contours of the shell. The cars, like the engine, had an ovoid cross-section and were flush on the exterior. All moldings, sills, pipes and vents that might protrude and create vacuums were eliminated. In keeping with the known laws of aerodynamics, the rear lounge car was tapered (fig. 45), and large windows created a solarium.

Like his *Air Liner Number 4*, the train would offer the maximum of comfort and convenience. The design featured air-conditioning, panoramic windows and lightweight aluminum construction. Geddes was aware that on trial runs from New York to Washington the addition of air-conditioning had increased passenger revenues on the Baltimore and Ohio Railroad. For too long the railroad had sacrificed comfort for capacity; he insisted that situation must be reversed. Railroad cars ought to be as clean and pleasant as a hotel or an ocean liner for the feminine point of view could no longer be ignored.[18] Colors should be "cheerful, gay and inviting" and the interiors easy to keep clean. Geddes specified cork floors, bakelite tables, aluminum Venetian blinds and Monel metal trim throughout, with a prohibition against dirt-catching ornament.

Service would be par excellence: the crew would include valets, maids and barbers as well as a dining-car staff. Central communications would assure additional convenience:

> *The entire train is equipped with a telephone system which has its own switchboard operator. She is also general information clerk for the train. Meals can be ordered without leaving one's room and the dining-room steward can notify the passenger by telephone when a*

*table is available in the dining car. One can talk with passengers in other rooms and in other cars of the train, or make reservations for a bridge table in the lounge or day car.*[19]

For the businessman, Geddes planned a traveling office with three private compartments, a telegraph office, a ticker room and a Trans-lux projector. Here one of two public stenographers could be hired, the latest financial reports could be read and one's broker could be telephoned.[20] Thus occupied, the businessman would not feel travel time was wasted.

By 1933 the American Railway Association was studying the practicability of streamlining locomotives and rolling stock; tests were being conducted at the universities of Illinois and Wisconsin and at Purdue University. Edward Hungerford, the pageant-master of the railroads who produced several fairs and expositions, called the nation's rail system "a machine of machines. All correlating, all working to the same major purpose, the swift, safe, efficient movement of man and his goods over the face of a broad continent." [21] To that end, he reported, streamlined trains "capable of easily making more than one hundred miles an hour" were being planned.[22] At the same time, Martin Stevers was of the opinion that

*In the matter of speed, the prospects for matching the airplane are by no means so hopeless as they appear. In fact, the railroads could have gone far toward accomplishing this long ago, had they not clung so conservatively to their nineteenth-century equipment.*

47. Pullman Car and Manufacturing Company. The *City of Salina.* 1934. (*Union Pacific Railroad Museum Collection.*)

*Just one thing was needed—streamlining their trains—for surprising though it may seem, air resistance is what limits present-day train speeds.*[23]

With public interest aroused, the race was on to be the first to put a high-speed streamliner into passenger service. Otto Kuhler and the American Car and Foundry engineers worked feverishly to complete plans for a lightweight, articulated three-unit train to satisfy Union Pacific's interest in an "egg-shaped train." The contract was lost to Pullman Car and Manufacturing of Chicago which delivered the *City of Salina* (fig. 47) on February 12, 1934. Some called it a "monster airplane fuselage on wheels," but the Union Pacific considered it "Tomorrow's Train, Today!"[24] The power unit, the *M.10,000*, contained an engine room with its 12-cylinder, 600-horsepower engine, a railway post office compartment, a baggage compartment and air-conditioning equipment. The middle unit shared a four-wheel truck with each of the other units and seated sixty passengers in four-position reclining chairs. The trailing unit included washrooms,

48. Interior of the *City of Salina.* (*Union Pacific Railroad Museum Collection.*)

49. Rear view, *City of Salina.* (*Union Pacific Railroad Museum Collection.*)

seating for fifty-six and, in the tail, a buffet-kitchen where light meals were prepared for service at the passenger's chair.

An "exhaustive" study was made of data from aircraft wind-tunnel tests, but in order to determine the effect of the ground plane below the train, a number of wooden scale models were tested in the tunnels at the University of Michigan.[25] As a result of these findings, the trucks (wheel units) were shrouded and the units connected with rubber sheeting to close gaps. Doors and windows were set flush with the body, which was three feet lower than conventional cars. Extruded aluminum was used to frame the tubular bodies. Air-conditioning, indirect lighting, safety-glass windows and rubber-cushioned trucks added to passenger comfort and safety. As a result of the streamlining and the lower center of gravity, operating costs were comparatively low, and the 204-foot *City of Salina* could attain 110 mph, cruising at 90 mph.

The interior color scheme was simple. Overhead, the vaulted ceiling was white; this progressed through shades of light blue to a dark blue below the black Micarta windowsills. Horizontal strips of aluminum sep-

50. The E. G. Budd Manufacturing Co. The Burlington *Zephyr*. 1934. (*Burlington Northern Railroad Photo*.)

arated the blue bands. Seats were upholstered in a golden-brown tapestry and the arms set upon a curve of aluminum tubing (fig. 48).[26] For maximum visibility, the exterior was enameled in golden brown along the skirting and on the canopy above the windows. Side panels were canary yellow (fig. 49), as bright and clear as the train's special loud siren. The train was rushed from Omaha to Washington, D.C. and inspected by President Franklin D. Roosevelt. It continued on a 13,000-mile tour through twenty-two states, making sixty-eight stops without a mishap. At the 1934 Century of Progress Exposition in Chicago, over a million and a half potential customers toured the first streamliner, taking home souvenir coins made of the special alloy developed for the train's body. When the train was scrapped for war materials in 1942 it had rolled up nearly 900,000 miles and grossed over $700,000 in revenues.[27]

The Chicago, Burlington and Quincy Railroad was a close second in the competition. Its entry, the *Zephyr* (fig. 50), was delivered two months after the *City of Salina*. The E. G. Budd Manufacturing Company had perfected a method of welding stainless steel which reduced the weight of structural members. The Budd-built *Zephyr* was also a three-unit streamliner with an engine-baggage car, a coach and an observation car with an elliptical tail (fig. 51). Unlike its brightly colored competitor, it was finished in gleaming stainless steel, its corrugated sides emphasizing the

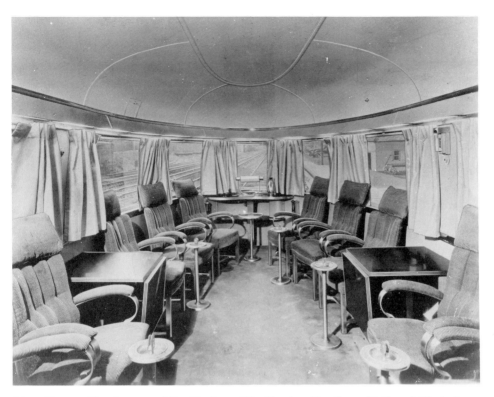

51.  Observation lounge of the *Zephyr.* (*Burlington Northern Railroad Photo.*)

low horizontal lines and the sense of forward movement. It demonstrated the utility of railcars on May 26, 1934, with a nonstop dusk-to-dawn trip from the Mile High City to the Windy City. The *Zephyr* covered those 1,015.4 miles in 13 hours, 4 minutes and 58 seconds, an average of 77.6 mph.[28] Fuel costs were remarkably low—31 cents per mile—even though a portion of the energy was consumed by the air-conditioning units. Like the Union Pacific streamliner it was sent on a promotional tour, and in six months more than two million people had seen the *Zephyr.*

Renamed the *Pioneer Zephyr* in 1936, it was joined that year by the *Denver Zephyr* with its two-unit engine, a baggage-cocktail lounge, two coaches, a diner, three sleeping cars, an eight-unit bedroom car and an observation car with swivel seats (figs. 52, 53). Service from Chicago to Minneapolis was provided by the *Twin Zephyr.* All three featured interiors by the architect Paul Cret, who decided upon "bright color accented with lines of chromium or stainless steel mouldings." [29] Cret approved of the "striking effect" of the exterior, where black enameled letters contrasted with the polished steel. The general appearance was modern and gave rise to engine and car names like the *Silver King, Silver Queen* and the *Silver State.* Later Zephyr service incorporated General Motors diesel-electrics and Budd coaches of types that became standard equipment on many railroads, but for most of the thirties the early *Zephyrs*

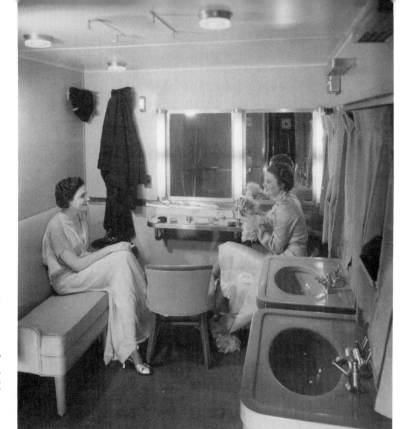

52.  Paul Cret and the E. G. Budd Manufacturing Company. The *Denver Zephyr*. 1936. Ladies lounge. (*Burlington Northern Railroad Photo.*)

53.  The *Denver Zephyr* Lounge Car. 1936. (*Burlington Northern Railroad Photo.*)

54.   Otto Kuhler. The Gulf, Mobile and Northern *Rebel*. 1934. (*Courtesy Otto Kuhler.*)

were unique in appearance and as memorable as the Douglas *DC–3*. Together with the *City of Salina*, they had rekindled interest in rail travel and shown that it could be clean, comfortable and enjoyable.[30] In short, they fulfilled many of Norman Bel Geddes's predictions.

The relative low cost of diesel-electric railcars made possible the custom designing of special units for particular applications, and a variety of forms resulted. No longer were trains the sole province of a few builders. The Gulf, Mobile and Northern Company's *Rebel* was, in 1934, the first lightweight, high-speed streamliner to operate in the southern states (fig. 54). That year the Pullman Car and Manufacturing Company began testing an experimental single-unit railcar, the *Railplane,* designed by William Stout. The Goodyear-Zeppelin Corporation made its entry in 1935 with the *Comet* (fig. 55). The New York, New Haven and Hartford Railroad needed a high-speed train for frequent trips between Boston and Providence. Goodyear, chosen because of its specialized knowledge of streamline forms and great experience in fabricating light metals, utilized the stressed-skin or monocoque type of construction. As project director Dr. Karl Arnstein explained it, the entire skin of the roof, side walls and bottom acted as one of the main load-carrying elements of the structure.[31] Particularly unique was the *Comet*'s symmetry; the sixty-four passenger coach was flanked

55. The Goodyear-Zeppelin Corporation. The New York, New Haven and Hartford *Comet*. 1935. (*Courtesy Goodyear Aerospace Corporation.*)

by two power units, each seating forty-eight passengers. Because the dense New England rail traffic prevented turnarounds, the train was made to operate from either end. N.Y.N.H.&H. officials declined Goodyear's suggested name ("Rail Zeppelin"). The *Comet*'s unusual helmetlike face became a familiar sight on the line, making its forty-three mile run in slightly less than one hour. The *Comet*'s smooth appearance was marred only by its scaly reptilian skin (embossed for greater strength) and the innumerable necessary but distracting rivets.

In hindsight, the diesel-electrics represented such an economic advantage that one would expect an immediate and systematic replacement of steam engines. Consider the thousands of leaking water towers and rotting coal towers that had to be maintained, often in remote outposts of the rail empires. The hauling of coal to supply points, the pumping of water and the removal of tons of ashes—all drained considerable energy from the system. Crews worked around the clock, banking fires in steam engines-in-waiting to keep the steam pressure up to a minimal level. There was a constant struggle against rust and alkaline corrosion and the never-ending rituals of lubricating massive bearings, pistons and crankrods. Engine repair shops were gargantuan caves where the disassembly and reassembly of great steel parts, the welding of boilers and the forging of makeshift parts—all enacted amid showers of sparks and thunderous noise —was a spectacle worthy of Vulcan.

All of this inefficiency, filth and squalor could be remedied by the diesel. With smooth riding, fast, air-conditioned closed trains, even Phoebe Snow could arrive at her destination without a speck of soot on her white dress. And the new engines *looked* clean and shiny. But immediate diesel-ization was not possible. There was a conservative element in management (as among the passengers) who thrilled to a steam whistle, spoke of "iron men" and began their banquet speeches with *"Breathes there the man, with soul so dead . . . ?"* Romantics aside, even the hard-nosed could not ignore the tremendous investment in steam equipment, the numbers of workers dependent upon steam for their sustenance or the difficulty in financing the diesel conversion during the Depression. No overnight changes were to take place, but until the last steam engine was replaced it could at least be given an aerodynamic facelift for whatever technological advantage, and public-relations gains might be had. The way was shown by a young man studying at a midwestern college.

For his senior thesis in mechanical engineering at Cleveland's Case School of Applied Science (now Case Western University), undergraduate Norman F. Zapf chose to test the feasibility of streamlining a 4-6-4 Hudson-type engine.[32] Zapf was familiar with Tietjen's work at Westinghouse and with tests underway at Canada's National Research Laboratories, where J. J. Green had, since 1931, been applying drag-reducing shells to steam engines.

Zapf concluded from wind-tunnel tests on scale models (with and without shrouds) that at a typical top passenger-train speed of 75 miles per hour, streamlining reduced drag by 91 percent; with crosswind effects the results were even better. By his calculations, a standard steam engine would expend 350 horsepower *more* than a streamlined locomotive with both operating at top speed, and his graphs showed that streamlining offered some power savings even below 50 mph. The model shroud (fig. 56) was altered to facilitate maintenance on the running gear (fig. 57).

Nearly all of Zapf's suggestions were incorporated in America's first streamlined steam engine, the *Commodore Vanderbilt* (fig. 58), which rolled out of the New York Central's Albany shops in December of 1934. A three-year-old engine had been given a black zephyr-like shroud from which only the handrails protruded. A trough along the top channeled smoke up and over the cab. Preliminary tests indicated that in the 70 to

56.  Norman F. Zapf holding a wind-tunnel form that proved much more efficient than the conventional steam engine represented by the scale model. (*Courtesy Mildred Zapf.*)

110 mph range, streamlining would effect a 2½ to 12 percent increase in pulling capacity over standard engines.[33] The *Commodore Vanderbilt* was quickly assigned to one section of the prestigious *20th Century Limited* operating between New York and Chicago.

57.  The final version of Zapf's test model was made practical and attractive. (*Courtesy Mildred Zapf.*)

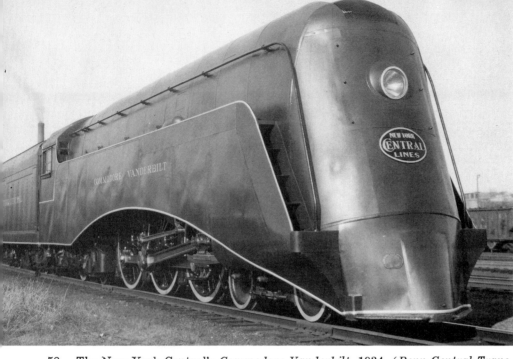

58.  The New York Central's *Commodore Vanderbilt*. 1934. (*Penn Central Transportation Company Photo.*)

Otto Kuhler designed a similar zephyrlike shroud for the all-new *Hiawathas*. The Milwaukee Road had to compete with the Burlington's *Twin Cities Zephyr* and the Chicago and North Western's *400*, both planned for 1935. Speed was all-important, but a low-power fixed-forma-

59.  Otto Kuhler. The Milwaukee Road's *Hiawatha*, pulled by Engine Number *2*. 1935. (*Chicago, Milwaukee, St. Paul and Pacific Railroad Company Photo.*)

tion train did not fit the Milwaukee Road's plans. High-power diesels fit for revenue service simply did not exist; steam was a viable solution. The American Locomotive Company created two new oil-burning 4-4-2 "Atlantic" engines with huge 84-inch drivers and enough power to assure 100 mph service.[34] Kuhler's simple shroud, determined by wind-tunnel tests, was finished in light gray with black along the top and an orange band bordered in maroon, the colors extending to the tender and along the all-new welded steel passenger cars (fig. 59). Chromium "wings" added a Deco note to the front, and golden letters adorned the tender and cars. The two *Hiawathas* began service in May 1935, reducing the 411-mile Chicago-Milwaukee-Minneapolis run from nine or ten hours to six and a half including fourteen stops en route.[35]

The *Hiawathas'* success forced an increase from seven- to nine-car trains after just sixteen months.[36] The new cars were distinguished by horizontal ribs, and when the original engines were replaced by larger "Hudson" types, Kuhler incorporated the ribs into the tender (fig. 60) and increased the horizontal effect with colored stripes that matched Wisconsin's autumn landscape. Side skirting was restricted, exposing the drivers. The newer engines topped 100 mph in daily service, and on one occasion a *Hiawatha* train *averaged* 120 mph over a five-mile stretch.[37] That kind of record attracted customers and gave the Milwaukee Road a new image now personified by the colorful engines—named for Longfellow's "swift of foot" Indian who could outrun his own arrow. Later engines sported prancing braves, angular Hiawathas painted on the tenders in zigzag designs which were seen in Sioux Falls, Tomahawk, Minocqua, Red Wing and other Indian-named towns.

The zephyr-styled shroud was the quickest and simplest way to convert a steam engine, and many railroads refurbished old engines in their

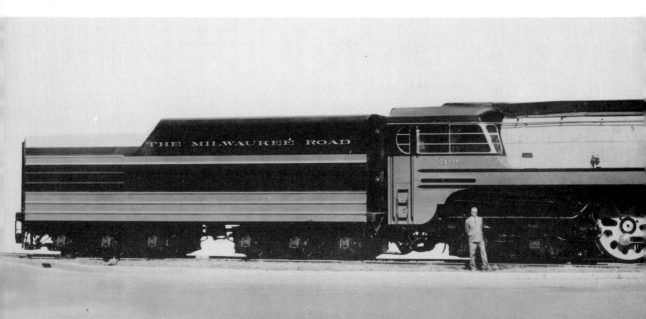

61. Henry Dreyfuss. The New York Central *Mercury*'s engine. 1936. (*Penn Central Transportation Company Photo.*)

own shops with the chief engineer as stylist. When the Burlington experienced some mechanical breakdowns with the *Zephyrs* in 1937, an older S-4 Hudson, number *3002,* was outfitted with a stainless-steel shroud with corrugations to match the train. Renamed *Aeolus* after the Greek god of the winds, it joined the *Zephyr* and *Pegasus* diesels only to be dubbed "Big Alice the Goon," a nickname it never overcame.[38] The two Reading Line *Crusaders,* revamped 4-6-2 "Pacifics" built in 1918, were similar to the *Aeolus.* They pulled the first steam-powered stainless-steel streamliners in the east, operating between Jersey City and Philadelphia.

Henry Dreyfuss designed one of the more restrained forms of the zephyr types. The New York Central *Mercury* of 1936 (fig. 61) featured

60. Otto Kuhler. Milwaukee Road Engine Number *100.* 1938. (*Courtesy Otto Kuhler.*)

disk drivers with painted "white-walls" that were illuminated at night by concealed spotlights. Its wraparound parallel molding had become one of the hallmarks of the streamlined style, perhaps because it suggested the trail of a projectile or the "speed whiskers" used by cartoonists to denote motion. Dreyfuss' design was bulky but uncluttered and neatly accented. The two K-5 "Pacifics," like their seven-car trains, were rebuilt from older equipment. Nevertheless, Dreyfuss called the *Mercurys* a "turning point in railroad design" because they were "the first streamliners done as a unit, inside and out, integrating everything from locomotives to dinner china." [39]

62. Raymond Loewy atop Engine *3768*. 1936. (*Raymond Loewy/William Snaith, Inc.*)

Most of the streamlined steam engines of the first half of the Streamlined Decade were frank imitations of the *Zephyr*, simple hull-like shrouds, rounded or slanted back at the front with gently sloping sides interrupted only by skirting hanging from the running boards and a set of steps on either side of the front. After 1935 several engines were designed that more closely resembled the cradled torpedo of Kuhler's 1928 sketches. The cylindricality of the boiler was emphasized, an approach that more nearly revealed its function as a steam engine. Running skirts were retained and the smokestack, the steam and sand domes, and other equipment atop the boiler were hidden in a narrow hood, giving a less bulky look than the zephyr-type shrouds. An effort was made to blend boiler, pilot, dome hood, skirts, cab and the tender with organic contours and horizontal accents. The tender matched the train and was often coupled to the all-weather cab with drag-reducing rubber or canvas bellows.

An early example of this type was Kuhler's bullet-nosed engine no. *5304* of 1935, a rich blue-and-gold torpedo type used to pull the *Royal Blue*, the Baltimore and Ohio's finest New York-to-Washington passenger train.[40] Concentric gold rings around the recessed headlamp and the cantilevered steps on each side of the pilot added to a refined design marred only by the line's emblem, the Capitol dome. The B & O continued to rebuild conventional equipment along Kuhler's design until 1946 when Ms. Olive Dennis, the line's first woman civil engineer, designed the *Cincinnatian*.[41]

Raymond Loewy designed the first Pennsylvania Railroad engine of the torpedo type in 1936. A single K-4 "Pacific" engine was remodeled after more than a hundred wind-tunnel tests at New York University on clay models indicated a 33⅓ percent reduction in wind resistance was possible.[42] An airfoil plate atop the dome hood deflected smoke over the cab, "thoroughly vindicating wind-tunnel results." Low skirts concealed the running gear and horizontality was emphasized by strips of stainless steel inlaid around the pilot and along the sides of the engine and tender. A winged Pennsy keystone in silver and red adorned the nose (fig. 62); silver and gold lettering, numerals and stripes enhanced the dark bronze color of the shroud. Engine *3768* pulled the *Broadway Limited* mainly between Chicago and Fort Wayne. After three years' service, it was put on display at the 1939 New York World's Fair.

The Pennsylvania Railroad began as early as 1905 to convert portions of the line to electric power.[43] Near the end of the 1920s, areas around New York and around Philadelphia were served by electric trains operated from an 11,000-volt overhead catenary system, and plans were

63.   Raymond Loewy. The Pennsylvania Railroad *GG–1* engine. (*Raymond Loewy/ William Snaith, Inc.*)

made to connect the two cities. The Philadelphia-to-Trenton section was started by 1930 and three years later service from Philadelphia to New York began. Two new engines were then being tested, the *R–1*, a rigid framed 4-8-4 unit with eight drivers, and the *GG–1*, an articulated unit having a symmetrical 4-6-0 + 0-6-4 wheel arrangement with twelve drivers. The latter was chosen for main-line service and the construction of fifty-seven locomotives was authorized. In cooperation with PRR engineers, Raymond Loewy designed a partially streamlined superstructure (fig. 63). The smooth shell resulted from welding rather than riveting panels onto the frame. The *GG–1* was symmetrical, with the cab in the center, and made to operate in either direction. The cab, hoods and side panels were joined with organic contours, the sloping hood necessitated by visibility factors. On most units five parallel gold stripes curved down to points at each end, enhancing the basic form. The *GG–1s* represented a considerable departure from earlier boxy and cluttered electric engines. When the electrification was extended to Washington in 1935, the *GG-1s* began pulling the *Congressional Limiteds*, the first trains in regular electric operation between New York and Washington.

Otto Kuhler began designing red and black engines for the Lehigh Valley Railroad in the late 1930s. To engine *2102*, which pulled the *John Wilkes* between Wilkes-Barre and New York, he added vertical fins around the stack and extended cantilevered pilot steps completely around the front skirting (fig. 64). These wing-like additions underscored the aeronautical origins of streamlining. He used them again on a Milwaukee Road solarium car in which the fins acted as sunshades while suggesting motion (fig. 65).

One of the finest of the torpedo-type streamlined steam engines was designed in 1938 by Henry Dreyfuss to haul the new *20th Century Limited*.

64. Otto Kuhler. Lehigh Valley's Engine Number *2102*. 1940. (*Courtesy Otto Kuhler.*)

Both engine and train, interior and exterior, were built new to Dreyfuss' specifications. (The exterior was painted in bands of gray with stripes of white and silver.) The New York Central had been developing a fleet of J series 4-6-4 "Hudsons" since 1927, including the Zapf-designed *Commodore Vanderbilt;* the remaining 264 engines were not streamlined.

65. Otto Kuhler and Karl F. Nystrom. *Hiawatha* observation car. 1937. (*Courtesy Otto Kuhler.*)

The ten engines built to Dreyfuss' design completed the roster at 275 units.[44] The new engines had a bold assertive appearance (fig. 66) that suggested power and speed without resort to color patterns, symbolic wings or other painted embellishments. The design was made harmonious through the repetition of circular and cylindrical elements neatly blended with the swelling form of the pilot. The nose, a pure hemisphere, was pierced by an extended headlamp and bisected by a sturdy fin, giving something of the look of a Trojan helmet.[45] The front coupler was hidden behind a panel and the pilot steps were recessed as pockets. Those engines fitted with Scullin double-disk drivers presented the simplest and most pleasing overall appearance. The engines were handsomely proportioned and neatly detailed. They blended beautifully with their trains (fig. 67), which were among the finest and fastest in railroad history. The engines were emblematic of speed and power combined with aerodynamic efficiency. Charles Sheeler, the Precisionist painter-photographer, selected the engine as one of six subjects for a series titled "Power" published in *Fortune* magazine.[46] His painting *Rolling Power* (1939) focused on the complex geometry

66. Henry Dreyfuss. Engine *5450*. 1938. (*Penn Central Transportation Company Photo.*)

of drivers, siderods and pistons and their attendant cranks and levers (fig. 68).

The interior of the new *20th Century Limited* has been described as stately but antiseptic.[47] Indeed, it was Dreyfuss who used the word "cleanlining" to describe his design strategy, and his work, like that of the other leading designers, was consistent with the machine aesthetic of purified, pristine forms that had developed in Europe earlier. A comparison of Dreyfuss' observation car (fig. 69) with a slightly earlier lounge car on the Frisco Lines (fig. 70) demonstrates the transition from the elegantly ornamental Art Deco decor to a severe but refined Moderne style. Without its passengers the *20th Century Limited* car may have appeared a bit inhospitable, but it had the virtue of simplicity and orderliness. There could be no hiding spilt coffee or ashes on those surfaces; one *knew* they were clean.

The lounge car was subdivided with enameled metal pillars trimmed in horizontal bands of chrome echoing the slats in the Venetian blinds. Built-in lamps repeated the forms in the pillars. Dreyfuss intended to re-

67. Henry Dreyfuss. The *20th Century Limited*. 1938. (*Penn Central Transportation Company Photo.*)

68.  Charles Sheeler. *Rolling Power*. 1939. Oil on canvas, 15 × 30 in. (*Smith College Museum of Art.*)

69.  Henry Dreyfuss. Observation car on the *20th Century Limited*. (*Penn Central Transportation Company Photo.*)

70. A lounge car of 1934 on the Frisco Lines. (*St. Louis–San Francisco Railway Photo.*)

create the atmosphere of a fine club with restful colors and club chairs. The diner (fig. 71) was bright and clean, uncrowded and decorated only with mirrors and polished metal. Diffused lighting gave the effect of a cool, shadowless atmosphere. There is something very efficient and businesslike about such a design that indicates the railroads were once again taking the passengers seriously.

The Santa Fe's only streamlined steam engine, number *3460*, was built in 1937; its shrouding added four tons of weight to the engine and one ton to the tender. Although technically in the same class as the New York Central's "Hudson" engines, the A.T. & S.F. *3460* series (nos. *3460–3465*) were larger and pulled longer trains over greater distances. Engine *3460* emerged from the Baldwin Locomotive Works with a dark blue undercarriage and running gear and a light blue torpedo-type superstructure (fig. 72). The two hues were separated by a band of stainless steel, and aluminum paint on the driver hubs and tires completed the scheme. The engine became known as the "Blue Goose," and its 84-inch diameter drivers suited it to high-speed trains like the *Chief* and the *Grand Canyon Limited*.[48] Bits and parts of the shroud were gradually removed to facilitate maintenance, a typical fate for streamlined steam engines.

The Santa Fe's finest passenger train, the *Super Chief*, was designed to compete in appearance and performance with Burlington and Union Pacific streamliners, but the impetus for the construction of the diesel-powered fleet came from the desert itself. The right-of-way in New Mexico and Arizona was too arid to slake the thirst of the *Blue Goose* (and larger steam passenger engines), and the Santa Fe had to haul and store millions of gallons of water at a cost of forty cents per thousand

71. Henry Dreyfuss. Dining Car on the *20th Century Limited.* (*Penn Central Transportation Company Photo.*)

72. Baldwin Locomotive Works. Santa Fe Railroad's Engine *3460*. 1937. (*Atchison, Topeka and Santa Fe Railroad Company Photo.*)

gallons.[49] Diesels provided the solution and it was decided that the *Super Chief* would be initiated with two blunt-nosed diesel units and conventional coaches until an all-new streamlined train could be designed and built. The Electro-Motive Corporation provided a new engine type for the job and painted them in two shades of blue with olive and scarlet red (fig. 73). Raymond Loewy called the scheme "baroque camouflage . . . meant

73. The Santa Fe *Super Chief* hauled by "Amos 'n Andy" in 1936. (*Atchison, Topeka and Santa Fe Railroad Company Photo.*)

for visibility," [50] but the boxy twin-unit engine, which came to be known as "Amos 'n' Andy," performed well, cutting the east-bound schedule by more than fifteen hours in May 1936. The high speeds were attained with sheer force rather than aerodynamic efficiency.

Meanwhile the Santa Fe assigned the design and construction of the stainless-steel coaches to Paul Cret and the Edward Budd Company. Then Dean of the University of Pennsylvania School of Architecture, Cret chose to outfit the interior of the *Super Chief* with thematic motifs rather than duplicate the polished "machine" style he had applied to the *Zephyrs*. Because the route was laid in the territory of the Pueblo Indians, their traditional motifs were adapted to the decor and the more luxurious cars were named after several of the Pueblos: *Isleta, Laguna, Acoma, Cochiti, Oraibi* and *Taos*.[51] In the observation car (fig. 74), the colors were, according to Cret,

74. Honeymoon on the all-new *Super Chief* of 1937. (*Atchison, Topeka and Santa Fe Railroad Company Photo.*)

*. . . those of the Pueblo—the brownish red tones taken from the old pottery, with notes of the bright blues, the blacks and the "bayetta" red found in the old weavings. The ceiling lighting was a "plumed serpent" from the Hopi tribal snake festival, to be lighted by blue lamps of low voltage. On the wall were painted representations of the ceremonial dolls of the Pueblo tribes.[52]*

To add a note of authenticity to the woven fabrics, the Jacquard looms were programmed to drop an occasional stitch as might be found in a Navajo rug.

As a backdrop for what might be called these Pueblo Deco motifs, a variety of exotic wood veneers were used as paneling. Bubinga, Macassar Ebony, Avodire, Zingana and Brazilian Rosewood were but a few of the

75. The Super Chief's *Acoma* lounge car of 1937. (*Atchison, Topeka and Santa Fe Railroad Photo.*)

woods "drawn from the four corners of the world." The *Acoma* lounge car (fig. 75) was paneled in Zingana from West Africa. Behind the bar was an inlaid-wood mural based very roughly on the image of a Kachina figure. The *Acoma*'s decor also included hanging Navajo rugs, pigskin couches and window shades trimmed in red, silver and tan Navajo patterns. "Authentic" sand paintings and sepia-toned photo murals of Indian weavers and shepherds also adorned the interiors.

When the streamlined version of the *Super Chief* began operation in 1937, it was perhaps the most sumptuous train of the decade and the service was comparable. In the *Cochiti* diner one could sample of the Swordfish Steak Sauté, Meunière with Capers for 75 cents, the Poached Tranche of Salmon, au Vin Blanc for 70 cents, or share a Sirloin Steak for Two for less than three dollars—all at 1937 prices.[53] Passengers need not have sat up all night on the early *Super Chiefs:* there were 104 comfortable beds in various compartments, bedrooms and convertible section cars. Every effort was made to make the 2,227-mile Chicago-to-Los Angeles trip—a bit under forty hours—as pleasurable as one could reasonably expect. To that end, the Santa Fe had spent about $942,000 on the first streamlined *Super Chief,* including the engines and sixteen cars.[54] No doubt the air conditioning, barber shop, fine wines and foods, and radio and recorded music in every room added to the train's considerable reputation.

When streamlined steam and diesel engines were introduced with new or remodeled trains they were often christened with names associated with speed. *Mercury, Zephyr, Blue Comet, Rocket, Silver Meteor, Flying Yankee, Electroliner, South Wind, Streamliner* and similar names graced the schedules of the thirties. Stylish, comfortable and convenient interiors and clean, colorful exteriors conveyed the intent of railroads to present a modern appearance. The aerodynamic profile of the engines, the smooth sides and rounded tops of the cars and the tapered rear of the train provided an appropriate symbolic form for the modernization of rail travel.

By the end of the decade the railroads had become concerned that the public believe they were efficiently and progressively managed. A survey of 1941 revealed that eighty-two percent of passengers were impressed with five major improvements: (1) faster, larger, more powerful locomotives; (2) streamlined trains; (3) diesel power or electrification; (4) more comfortable and attractive coaches; and (5) air conditioning.[55] These included some of the recommendations made by Norman Bel Geddes and Otto Kuhler a decade earlier. *Railway Age* noted that

76. American Locomotive Company. The Chicago and Northwestern's Engine Number *4001*. 1938. (*Chicago and Northwestern Transportation Company Photo.*)

*It is significant that all these improvements have been made partly or entirely in passenger service, and that they are all of kinds that make a* physical *impression of one sort or another on the observer. . . . It was things that an overwhelming majority could* see *and* feel *that had influenced their opinion.*[56]

By November of 1941, the total number of streamlined trains in regular service had increased to 121. A pictorial and statistical review implied that most of these were pulled by diesels.[57] Those built by the Electro-Motive Division of General Motors seemed to have been the most common in the late 1930s. Yet streamlined steam engines continued to appear until 1950. The same year (1938) that the American Locomotive Company delivered six streamlined "Hudsons" to the Milwaukee Road, they built nine similar engines for the Chicago and North Western (fig. 76). Engines *4001–4008* were put into service between Chicago and Omaha,

77.    Raymond Loewy. The Pennsylvania Railroad's *S–1*. Designed in 1937, built in 1938. (*Raymond Loewy/William Snaith, Inc.*)

78.    Raymond Loewy. Bar Lounge Car of the *Broadway Limited*. 1938. (*Raymond Loewy/William Snaith, Inc.*)

and were painted a dark Pullman green with gold lettering and striping. Two older "Pacific" engines were remodeled along the same lines in 1941 but were painted in bright green and yellow to match their trains, the Minnesota *400s*.[58]

The American Railway Association began testing steam locomotives in 1938 to determine what power was necessary to accelerate a thousand-ton passenger train to 100 miles per hour and maintain that speed on level track. The Pennsylvania Railroad was at the same time conferring with several engine builders on specifications for a locomotive to exceed that performance by 200 tons. The result was the "duplex," with two separate sets of pistons, cylinders, side rods and 84-inch drivers set in one rigid frame.[59] Over 140 feet long, the engine and tender occupied 23,000 cubic feet, and with a 100-mph top speed streamlining this enormous volume was an absolute necessity. Raymond Loewy cooperated with the PRR engineering staff in the design of an air-smoothed envelope not dissimilar

79. Raymond Loewy. The Bar in the *Broadway Limited*. 1938. ( *Raymond Loewy / William Snaith, Inc.*)

to engine number *3768* of 1936 but with an extended pilot cowl that covered a six-wheel pilot truck (fig. 77). The torpedo effect was more pronounced; the boiler had a sharper nose with an extended headlamp and a sharp horizontal ridge that disappeared into the sides. A bright metal strip extended this horizontal back to the cab. The side skirts were generally flat, interrupted only by the forms of the cylinders pressing from within. The *S-1* took over the task of hauling the *Broadway Limited,* which was also renovated. The interior of the train was designed to be comfortable and intimate to compete with air travel. Loewy used mirrors to double the apparent width of the car, carpeting and upholstered modern furniture to reduce the noise level, and air conditioning and soft music to make the journey more pleasant (figs. 78, 79).

The *S-1* was viewed by millions of visitors to the 1939 New York World's Fair where it operated under its own steam atop a treadmill.[60] Thereafter the million-pound engine pulled fast passenger trains from Chicago only as far as Crestline, Ohio: the length of its frame precluded its admission to the sharper curves near the Pittsburgh depot.

80.   Seaboard Air Line Shops. Engine Number *868.* 1940. (*Seaboard Coast Line Photo.*)

Among the oldest engines remodeled during the decade was the Seaboard's number *868* "Pacific," built in 1913 by the Richmond Locomotive Works. In 1940 number *868* and two sister locomotives were given zephyr-like shrouds finished in creamy yellow and olive drab with an orange waistband and wheels trimmed in yellow (fig. 80). The paint job matched the Seaboard Air Line's diesels and cars of the *Silver Meteor,* and the steam engines pulled that train in western Florida.[61]

For its various *Daylight* passenger trains the Southern Pacific ordered semi streamlined 4-8-4s from the Lima Locomotive Company. The first group of six were delivered in 1937 and had been designed by George McCormack and F. E. Russell, Sr.—both Southern Pacific employees. Assigned to the Los Angeles *Coast Daylight,* they managed the 470-mile run in 9¾ hours.[62] Like the twenty cars in the consist, the engines were painted orange, red and black. Later versions (fig. 81) had larger drivers and rotating Mars lights set in their silvery smokeboxes. The same fleet headed the inland *San Joaquin Daylight,* the *Lark,* and the *Shasta Daylight.*

Otto Kuhler streamlined a steam engine for the last time in 1941.

81. George McCormack and F. E. Russel, Sr. Southern Pacific Engine Number *4454.* 1941. (*Southern Pacific Transportation Company Photo.*)

Engine number *1380*, a 4-6-2 Pacific, had been built in the mid-twenties, one of a dozen. Curved steel segments were welded to form the shell, since earlier aluminum castings had cracked under the stress of the wind's buffeting. Kuhler's green-and-white torpedo shroud made it one of a kind (fig. 82). Only the arched cab window and ornate trailing truck frame hinted at its past. Like all Southern Railway engines of the prewar period, *1380* was well groomed and its bullet nose was to be seen at the head of the *Tennessean* between Washington and Monroe, Virginia from which point other engines hauled the nine coaches to Memphis.[63]

When, in 1865, Reverend Calthrop made an analogy between his "air-resisting train" and a shark's head, he intended a reference to nature's functionalism. Perhaps he was also expressing an idea not uncommon in the relationship of men and machines; that the latter are like living creatures with vitality and personalities, sometimes harnessed to useful ends but occasionally rebellious. In *Hard Times*, for example, Dickens likened the endless rocking of a factory machine to "the head of an elephant in a state of melancholy madness." [64] Samuel Clemens, who dearly loved the paddle-boat steamers, used one as a frightening villain that destroyed Huck's raft. As his character explains, ". . . all of a sudden she bulged out, big and scary, with a long row of wide-open furnace doors shining like red-hot teeth. . . ." [65] Locomotives have also been cast as literary monsters. In his novel *The Octopus*, Frank Norris describes the young protagonist, Presley, in a mood of reverie one starlit evening when suddenly

> *with a quivering of all the earth, a locomotive, single, unattached, shot by him with a roar, filling the air with the reek of hot oil, vomiting smoke and sparks; its enormous eye, Cyclopean red, throw-*

82. Otto Kuhler. Southern Railway Engine Number *1380*. 1941. (*Southern Railway System Photo.*)

83.   Springfield Shops of the St. Louis–San Francisco Railway. Frisco Engine Number *1026*. (*St. Louis–San Francisco Railroad Photo.*)

*ing a glare far in advance, shooting by in a sudden crash of confused thunder; filling the night with the terrific clamour of its iron hoofs.*[66]

Although many streamlined engines utilized the principles of organic or biomorphic forms, graphic resemblances were rare. The Lackawanna Railroad remodeled several steam engines in the thirties with a modicum of streamlining but added huge sheet-metal wings along the running boards. Otto Kuhler recalled asking the engineer how the wings were made to flap, recognizing that a too graphic symbol can be confusing.[67]

The St. Louis-San Francisco Railway created a fish-like form when it shrouded engine number *1026* (fig. 83). Eric Archer described the shape as "sinister." [68] An even closer semblance to nature can be seen in Raymond Loewy's *T–1* duplex locomotive of 1942 (fig. 84). Commonly called the "sharknose" *T–1*, the engine was the forerunner of a style of later diesels and bears comparison with a contemporary military airplane, the *P–40*. General Chennault's "Flying Tigers" had painted sharks' teeth and eyes on the cowling of their fighters (fig. 85) and had began to fly sorties over the Burma Road the year before the *T–1* was built. The locomotive also had a nautical air about it with its sharp "prow" and "portholes" in the pilot casing.

84. Raymond Loewy. The Pennsylvania Railroad's *T–1*. 1942. (*Raymond Loewy/ William Snaith, Inc.*)

85. The Curtiss *P–40* with psychographics by Claire Chennault's Flying Tigers squadron. 1942. (*Official U.S. Air Force Photo.*)

The public came to expect streamlined service, even during and after the Second World War. As one railway executive expressed it, "the streamliner is the answer to the passenger-traffic manager's prayer." [69] By 1943 most of the well-known streamliners, like the Illinois Central Railroad's *Green Diamond* (fig. 86), were earning 200 to 300 percent more than they had before the war. Those figures reflect a wartime boom economy, and passengers were generally military personnel or civilians engaged in defense work, but the trains' popularity continued to grow. The Norfolk and Western built engine *606* "in uniform" (fig. 87), since wartime shortages prohibited the use of steel for shrouding, but soon after V–J day it was streamlined to match its prewar sisters (fig. 88).

A comparison of engine *606*—one of five engines in its class—before and after streamlining points up the visual improvements that could be wrought. Without its shroud the engine was for most observers a confusion of pipes, valves, domes, rivets and hinges. One may not have understood their function but could still sense the resistance they represented

86.   Electro-Motive Division of General Motors. The *Green Diamond*. 1936. (*Courtesy Illinois Central Gulf Railroad.*)

to motion through air. The shroud presented a single comprehensible form very obviously suited to easy penetration. None of the fascination of the kinetic action was lost, for the running gear was still exposed. Below the skirts, the drivers and siderods *demonstrated* the engines' power; the superstructure above *symbolized* the speed that power could provide while conserving some of the energy generated.

The conversion of older, cluttered forms to smoother ones usually denoted improved mechanical performance. This was the case with the development of the modern streetcar. In 1929 the American Electric Railway Association formed among its executive members, presidents of several transit companies, the Presidents' Conference Committee.[70] The P.C.C. was allotted a half-million dollars and charged with the develop-

88.   Roanoke Shops of the Norfolk and Western Railway Co. Engine Number *606* (fancy). (*Norfolk and Western Railway Company Photo.*)

87.  Roanoke Shops of the Norfolk and Western Railway Co. Engine Number *606* (plain).  1944.  (*Norfolk and Western Railway Company Photo.*)

ment of a car embodying such new features as noiseless operation, higher operating speeds, smoother starting and stopping, riding comfort and greater riding appeal, all with maximum safety. The result was the *P.C.C.* car (fig. 89) still in use in many cities. The Chicago Surface Lines put prototypes of the cars in service in 1934 carrying passengers to the "Century of Progress" exposition. The improved design was not only more attractive but easier to maintain and it provided riders with better visibility and a smoother ride. Those improved were conveyed visually by the smooth new exteriors. The *P.C.C.* cars made the excitement of streamlined travel available on a daily basis to those who could not afford the longer ride on the glamorous *20th Century Limited* or the exotic *Super Chief.*

89.  St. Louis Car Co. The *P.C.C.* Car. (*Courtesy Chicago Transit Authority.*)

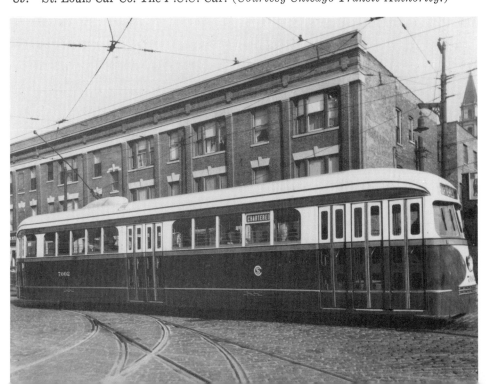

# VI.
# TERRANAUTICS:
# THE STREAMLINED
# AUTOMOBILE

## OPTIMISM RULES: THE TEARDROP CARS

"Today," wrote Norman Bel Geddes in 1932, "speed is the cry of our era, and greater speed one of the goals of tomorrow." [1] The potential for speed seemed to Geddes so great as to silence the skeptics. "Optimism rules. One hears the easy, offhand prediction that the motor car will attain five hundred and the airplane a thousand miles an hour, as though this were a matter of course!" [2] That optimism grew out of the application of aerodynamics to racing cars and the repeated breaking of land speed records. The transfer of aeronautical design principles to automobiles gave rise to more organic forms and began to take place in the late nineteenth century. This coincided approximately with the rise of the Art Nouveau movement which exalted natural forms. The Art Nouveau designer adapted the undulating fluid lines of vines and tendrils to architecture, furniture and the decorative arts. The "whiplash" motif became a unifying device for the new environment. It was a fresh, inventive and nonhistorical movement that created a dynamic aesthetic and sought to apply it every-where. When competitions were held in Paris in 1895 to encourage the

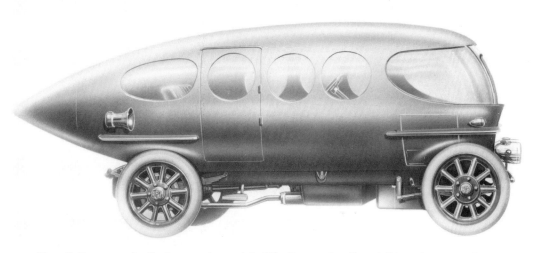

90.  Il Carrozzeria Castagna. A special *Alfa Romeo* for Count Ricotti. 1914. (*Courtesy Alfa Romeo, Milan.*)

design of beautiful automotive forms, the prize went to Pierre Selmersheim, whose wax maquette incorporated the principles of Art Nouveau design: an undulating profile, a sculptural organic form and the merging of forms with smooth curves. The jury was moved to liken it to a projectile which would cleave the air.[3] The body swept up from the ground, rippled over the front wheels and again over the passenger compartment, then rose again to a second level where the driver sat. With its many round-topped windows, the body looked more like a fancy shoe than a projectile.

Selmersheim's design was dictated more by taste than by aerodynamic necessities. As we have seen, the teardrop had been established by the end of the century as the ideal low-resistance form. The form inspired an early streamlined Italian car (fig. 90). Designed for a Count Ricotti by the coachbuilder Castagna, the body was adapted to a 1914 Alfa Romeo chassis. This bold experiment was in the spirit (if not to the letter) of aerodynamic design. Perhaps because of its size and added weight it was actually slower than standard Alfa Romeos.[4]

Under the Treaty of Versailles, Germany was forbidden to develop and build powered airplanes and airships.[5] With a large investment in aeronautical test facilities, the defeated nation turned its attention to unpowered gliders and to the streamlining of automobiles. The pioneer aircraft designer and builder Edmund Rumpler introduced his *Tropfenwagen* ("teardrop car") in 1921. It was a lightweight enclosed car based upon his intuitive understanding of aerodynamics. It underwent studies at Gustave Eiffel's aerodynamic laboratory in Auteuil, France. Although its profile was rather boxy, it looked like a teardrop when viewed from above. The front was rounded and the flat sides came together in a vertical edge at the rear. The windows and roof were not blended with the rest of the body, but Rumpler had reduced drag with solid-disk wheels, an enclosed radiator and airfoil fenders.[6]

The Hungarian engineer Paul Jaray was a significant figure in the history of the streamlined automobile. Jaray was chief of design and development at the Zeppelin airship works at Freidrichshafen from 1914 to

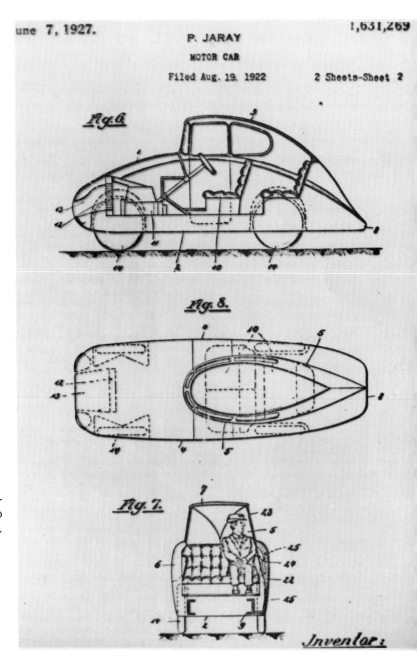

91. Paul Jaray. Patent Drawings for streamlined auto bodies. Filed 1922, issued 1927. (*Author's Collection.*)

1923, during which time the management made plans to design and build aerodynamically efficient auto bodies.[7] In 1921 Jaray and his assistant W. Klemperer began testing tenth-scale models in Zeppelin's new wind-tunnel test facility. Their efforts resulted in an application that year for the first German patent on the new form. The following year the Zeppelin works built a full-size prototype of the Jaray body and placed it on a Ley chassis. Coasting tests proved it to have about half the drag coefficient of the stock Ley auto.[8] Closed automobiles were rare in the early 1920s, and the Jaray-Ley car was sufficiently radical in appearance to further hinder its adoption.

Jaray formed the Stream-line Carriage Body Company in Zurich and the Jaray Streamline Corporation in the United States where he was awarded a patent on his designs in 1927.[9] He stated as his intention the reduction of the resistance to air "in the highest degree attainable" and the diminishing of the raising of dust by the vehicle.[10] To this end, "the spokes of the wheels have been enclosed; the whole car has received a low and slender shape, and quite especially the body has been shaped somewhat like a torpedo or like an airship body." [11] All this attention to the superstructure would gain little, unless something were done about protuberances, especially the mechanical equipment below the car. On the other hand, to completely enclose the car in a teardrop form would impede driver vision and make steering difficult. Jaray's solution was to use half a streamline form with the section plane parallel to the roadway (fig. 91). Above this form was added another section providing windows and a roof and "shaped conformably to the lower main portion, especially at its rear, and with special consideration to the guidance of the air." [12] Jaray claimed twelve variations of the body within his patent, maintaining that it was the first completely streamlined automobile.[13] During the next dozen years Jaray bodies were built on Dixi, Ley, Opel, Mercedes-Benz and Maybach chassis.

When Walter Gropius, director of the Bauhaus, designed a series of elegant but boxy automobile bodies for the Adler Company of Germany during the late 1920s, he chose to ignore the trend toward aerodynamic design. Design critic Reyner Banham sees this as a breaking of "the visual link" between the International Style and advancing technology.[14] Gropius's designs were handsome but "mechanically backward" in comparison with the 1930 Streamliners of Sir Charles Burney, the British aviation designer. Burney's rear-engine cars roughly approximated an airfoil shape with flat sides and fenders added (fig. 92).[15]

For Norman Bel Geddes, there was "a certain stirring kind of appeal" in the average passenger car of the early 1930s, but he felt that it

92. Sir Charles Burney. The Burney *Streamliner. Ca.* 1930. (*Courtesy Chilton Publications and Motor/Age.*)

would never "exert the same force of appeal that the projectile-like racing car does until it is designed in accord with the same functional principles."[16] The problem was partly that of financing the cost of tools and dies and partly the conservative nature of the auto industry. Manufacturers were content to give major emphasis to minor details, and the results were mediocre.[17] Bodies were still rectangular and "lacked conviction" because they were not sufficiently *organic.* The beauty of motor cars, said Geddes, would be inherent when they had evolved into the essential forms determined by their function. We would then admire them as we admire the swordfish, the seagull, the greyhound and the stallion, for then automobiles would reveal their purpose through their forms.[18]

In 1928 Geddes designed a functional car, and because he felt it could become a reality in five years he titled it *Motor Car Number Five.* He then proceeded to design four more cars, each further from the ideal but closer to a typical 1928 model. *Motor Car Number One* (achieved by a kind of reverse evolution) could be driven on the streets without attracting attention "other than casual admiration" although it incorporated several mechanical innovations and moderate streamlining.[19] It had been designed for the Graham-Paige Motor Car Company, but department heads there found it too extreme and the intervening Depression precluded expenditures on a test model.

Geddes then began a second series of cars with exterior shells "as near the drop form as possible."[20] *Motor Car Number Eight* (fig. 93a) of 1931 was designed on a 116-inch wheelbase, comparable to a Buick or Chrysler, but because of its interior arrangement it held eight passengers instead of five. The driver sat in the front and enjoyed maximum visibility. With the engine in the rear, the driveshaft was eliminated giving the car a low center of gravity. Furthermore, heat and fumes from the engine

93.  Norman Bel Geddes. *Motor Car Number 8*, 1931 (TOP); *Motor Coach Number 2*, 1931
(CENTER); and a patent model of 1934 (BOTTOM). (*From the work of Norman Bel Geddes at
the Hoblitzelle Theatre Arts Library, The Humanities Research Center, University of Texas,
by permission of the executrix Edith Lutyens Bel Geddes.*)

were less of a problem. A vertical fin offered stability. *Motor Coach Number Two* (fig. 93b) was similar in form but larger; the swelling curve of the shell accommodated a second deck. On the lower deck a steward would prepare light meals and beverages. Air conditioning, indirect lighting, music and magazines would add to passenger comfort.[21] In 1934 Geddes and his associates were awarded a patent on an eight-wheeled version of the car (fig. 93c). Like its predecessors it featured a vertical stabilizer that extended the aircraft metaphor to land vehicles.

Through a grant from the Daniel Guggenheim Fund of 1926, several universities were able to build experimental wind tunnels. Scale-model autos were tunnel tested at the University of Detroit in 1931, the University of Michigan in 1933 and at Stanford University in 1934.[22] Case School of Applied Science had a facility as early as 1932, and within two years students were testing models of smokestacks, automobiles (and teardrops) and streamlined ships and locomotives (see Chapter 5).[23] The U.S. Bureau of Standards was also testing model automobiles and in 1933 published results of tests on six different forms.[24] The scale models represented (1) a closed sedan and (2) a touring car (with its top up) of 1922 vintage, both with wire wheels, (3) a lighter sedan of 1928, equally boxy and upright but with disk wheels, and three streamlined models. These last three included (4) a "composite" sedan of 1933 with moderate streamlining, slanted grill and windshield and partially enclosed wheels, (5) a streamlined sedan resembling the Jaray patent design with the passenger compartment in the conventional position, and finally (6) an airfoil shape with flat sides and the driver and passengers moved to the front. The tests were run "in view of the possibility of obtaining improved fuel economy or higher speeds by streamlining an automobile body and the consequent trend of design in this direction." [25] The relative values of drag coefficient obtained for the models were considered an indication of the progress made in reducing air resistance during the decade preceding the tests. The composite 1933 sedan model showed a 25 percent decrease in drag coefficient over the boxy 1928 model. By eliminating protruding elements and enclosing the upper halves of the wheels, streamlined model 5 realized a 70 percent reduction over the 1928 model. The airfoil shape of model 6 achieved only a moderate decrease in drag over model 5.[26] The researcher concluded that while progress in reducing drag had been made, more would be possible but would require radical changes in mechanical design.

The state of the art of metallurgy was not sufficiently advanced for Buckminster Fuller to realize his *4D Zoomobile* (see Chapter 3). He decided instead to develop only the vehicle's land-travel capability, aware that the ground contact maneuvering problems of his "wingless fish" would prove more difficult than making it flyable.[27] He conducted wind-tunnel tests on a three-wheeled teardrop form with a V-shaped channel cut into the length of its belly. Fuller intended that at high speeds the tail would lift from the ground and the channel would stabilize the craft; a rudder would unfold from the upper side of the tail like an opera fan, to provide steerability.[28] Three prototype *Dymaxion Cars* were then built (fig. 94) from which Fuller gained driving experience in cross winds, in traffic, cornering, parking, accelerating and braking. As a result of this he considered himself better prepared than other designers for pioneering the first phases of this "new era transport." [29]

In 1933 Fuller contracted the services of Starling Burgess, famed naval architect and aeronautical engineer, and hired a crew of expert sheet-metal workers, machinists, woodworkers and former coachbuilders. In a rented building in Bridgeport, Connecticut, Fuller set up production facilities and began designing *Dymaxion Car Number One*.[30] The vehicle was shown publicly in July of that year and in October Fuller applied for a patent on its design.[31] "The invention relates to the construction of motor road vehicles," the application read, "whereby they are adapted to the economical operation resulting from full streamline formation and whereby other and independent advantages are obtained. . . ." [32] As a result of enclosing all of the chassis and part of the wheels in a smooth tapered envelope, Fuller is reported to have attained a speed of 120 miles per hour with a 90-horsepower engine; to do so with a conventional 1933 sedan would have required, by his estimate, a 300-horsepower engine.[33] Fuller claimed that the relative fuel consumption would be 30 percent less than a conventional car at 30 mph and 50 percent less at 50 mph.[34]

The two forward wheels were driven by a Ford V–8 engine located behind the passenger compartment (fig. 95). The third wheel was steerable which facilitated parking between other cars and provided a very tight turning circle.[35] As a safeguard against side collisions Fuller proposed a warning signal actuated by extreme rotation of the steering wheel. On *Dymaxion Cars Two* and *Three* he provided an overhead rear-looking wide-angled periscope to compensate for the lack of rear windows.

The *Dymaxion Car* developed alongside a racing sloop Burgess was building, and its construction reveals the transfer of marine technology (fig. 96). Not only did it have an overhead keel and ribs but the *Architectural Record* was moved to describe its bow, beam, cabin bunks and stern "rudder." [36]

The car created a sensation wherever it went. A representative of a group of British auto enthusiasts flew to Chicago to examine the *Dymaxion Car*. He was injured and his driver was killed when the *Dymaxion*

94. Richard Buckminster Fuller. *Dymaxion Cars One, Two* and *Three* (TOP TO
BOTTOM). 1933, 1934. (*Courtesy R. Buckminster Fuller.*)

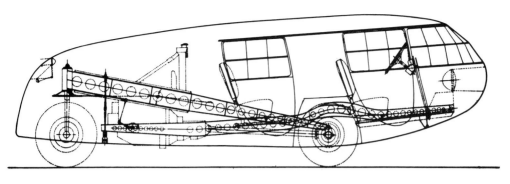

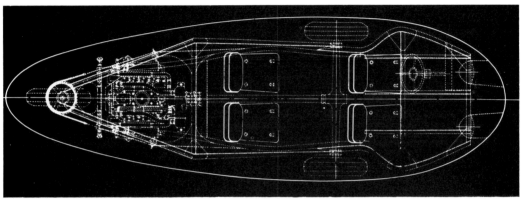

95.   Richard Buckminster Fuller. Elevation and plan of *Dymaxion Car Number One*. 1933. (*Courtesy R. Buckminster Fuller.*)

96.   Chassis and superstructure of *Dymaxion Car Number One* without its outer skin. (*Courtesy R. Buckminster Fuller.*)

*Car* collided with another car near the entrance to the 1933 Century of Progress Exposition. Sensational headlines referred to the vehicle as a "freak car" and pointed to its radical three-wheel design.[37] Although an investigation exonerated the *Dymaxion*'s design, the tragedy gave the car an undeserved reputation and the British group canceled their order for *Dymaxion Car Number Two,* completed in January of 1934. The third model was featured in the finale of Edward Hungerford's "Wings of a Century" pageant at the 1934 Century of Progress Exposition.[38]

The *Dymaxion Cars* represented the first reexamination of the automobile since its emergence as a motorized horse carriage. Fuller's use of streamlining for scientific reasons and his teardrop designs justified the similar forms promoted during the 1930s by American industrial designers. In light of the development of aerodynamics as they understood it, they had professed faith in an optimum form; streamlining was for them no passing fancy of the stylist. It represented changes they thought could and should come.

97. William Stout. The Stout *Scarab.* 1935. (*Courtesy Chilton Publications and Automotive Industries.*)

Not all designers endorsed the teardrop or felt that the strict application of aerodynamics to autos was useful. William B. Stout was a dissenter and a qualified critic. In 1922 he had built the first all-metal airplane in the United States and formed a company (later sold to the Ford Motor Co.) to build metal commercial planes. In 1926 he founded a passenger airline which was sold to United Aircraft.[39] Stout Engineering of Detroit was engaged in research on automotive, railroad and aircraft design and was consulted on the Pullman's experimental streamlined *Railplane.* Stout maintained that cross winds on a true teardrop tend to create a vacuum on its lee side; unlike an aircraft which can drift and correct for it, the auto must stay on the road. Streamlining, therefore, ought to result in forms more like the turtle or the crab than the bird.[40]

Stout's own design resembled a beetle. He unveiled his rear-engine *Scarab* (fig. 97) in 1935, a design he felt would have superior "roadability." The body was suspended at points well above the center of gravity, which gave it a tendency to pendulum or bank *into* a curve and therefore reduce the tendency to roll over.[41] Like the *Dymaxion Cars,* the interior of the *Scarab* was roomy and allowed passengers to move from the front to the rear, use a folding table, or rearrange the two rear chairs.[42] The body was an assembly of tubular steel hoops covered with sheet metal. Stout made no claims of wind-tunnel efficiency for he felt test methods gave ambiguous data. The real value of streamlining or "terranautics," as he called it, was that it had made the public aware of cleaner lines in automobiles: visual appeal was preliminary in increasing sales.[43]

The year the *Scarab* appeared (1935), Dr. Wunibald Kamm of Stuttgart was able to prove mathematically and empirically that the ideal streamlined form need not be extended back to a sharp point. The teardrop could be tapered as far as was practical and then truncated, leaving a nearly vertical flat wall at the rear. Smoke streams over wind-tunnel models of the K-form or Kamm-back design verified the effect: there was no increase in the drag coefficient without the pointed tail! So conditioned were the German aerodynamists to the teardrop that they treated news of this discovery as a joke.[44] Small wonder that American designers clung to their ideal. In 1937 the Lewis American Airways company unveiled their *Airmobile,* a three-wheeled front-wheel drive car with an air-cooled engine placed in the conventional forward position. The body was a compromise between the Jaray and *Dymaxion* designs.[45] Teague and W. D. Teague, Jr., designed a four-wheel teardrop car in 1938; Teague saw the gradual emergence of "the single simple form" that all high-speed vehicles would have. The future car would be "a sleek projectile," but subtle variations of plane, line and accents would still be possible.[46] In France, André Dubon-

98.   Andre Dubonnet. The *Dubonnet-Ford*. 1936. (*Courtesy Chilton Publications and Motor/Age.*)

net achieved a sense of sleekness with his experimental *Dubonnet-Ford* of 1936 (fig. 98). Although a stock Ford V-8 of 1936 was capable of only 81 mph, Dubonnet put the same engine in a teardrop body and achieved a top speed of 108 mph.

America's first industrial designers detected what they thought to be a natural and inevitable trend toward a single type. Raymond Loewy visualized this in his evolutionary chart of 1933 (fig. 99). At the 1939 New York World's Fair Loewy presented models and drawings of the automobile, taxi and motorcoach of the future (figs. 100–102). In the golden age of the airbrush the sheen of metal and glass became an essential feature of the industrial design presentation. Trails of mist behind the wheels and body enhanced the look of movement.

What he and his colleagues could not have predicted was that the auto of the immediate future would be as square as a shoebox, devoid of chrome and a glossy finish, loaded with protruding steps, handrails and brackets and would lack nearly all creature comforts. Nothing could be further from the glamorous ideal of the thirties than the military Jeep.[47] Had not World War Two intervened, the form of the modern automobile might have evolved just as Loewy predicted. But, as the lifestyle and needs of the nation changed, so too did the forms that filled those needs. The Jeep's brute appearance in countless wartime photos and newsreels reminded Americans of the stark realities being faced. In its own way it became a symbol of American ingenuity, adaptability and rugged endurance. Civilian passenger-car designs were held in abeyance "for the duration" (fig. 103).

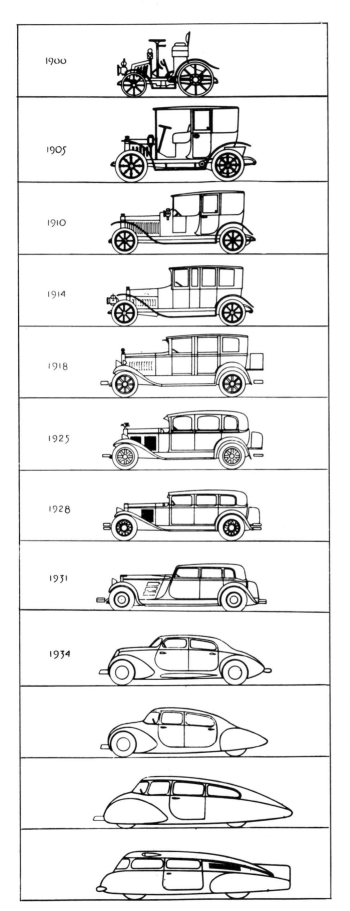

1900

1905

1910

1914

1918

1925

1928

1931

1934

99. Raymond Loewy. Evolution chart of automobiles. 1933. (*Raymond Loewy/ William Snaith, Inc.*)

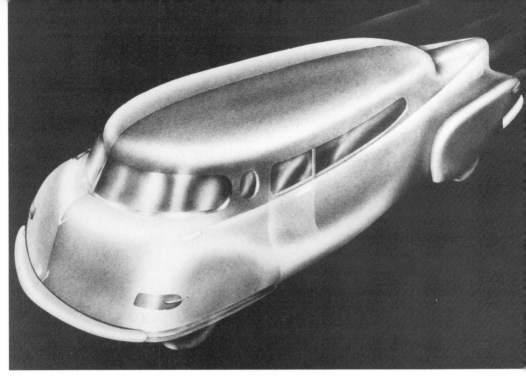

100. Raymond Loewy. The *Automobile of the Future*. 1938. (*Raymond Loewy/ William Snaith, Inc.*)

101. Raymond Loewy. The *Taxicab of the Future*. 1938. (*Raymond Loewy/William Snaith, Inc.*)

102. Raymond Loewy. The *Motorcoach of the Future*. 1938. (*Raymond Loewy/ William Snaith, Inc.*)

## THE CLASSICS

The very first automobile owners were men of means, and the urgent task of the early car builders was to provide them with reliable machines. As automobile travel became part of the patrician life-style, the traditions of the European coachbuilders were incorporated into the luxury car. Dignity was the watchword and it was expressed in fine materials and superb craftsmanship. "The tendency among custom coachmakers," reported one observer in 1923, "is to make the brougham a thing distinctly of the town, a formal, dignified, smart carriage, in keeping with the spirit of winter society and town functions." [48] These were formal vehicles for formal use and had "little to do with sweeping curves or with streamlines," or any of the "snappiness" preferred by the *parvenu*.[49]

A different viewpoint was expressed in a special 1927 edition of *The Little Review* which had just organized a "Machine-Age Exposition" of modern art, architecture and design. Editor Jane Heap wrote that "today the finest cars with their rhythmic coordination of lines induce a consciousness of velocity and motion even greater than their actual speed in miles per hour." [50] The age of the staid brougham had ended; the new custom car would be lower, longer and expressive. Among connoisseurs of fine automobiles, the name of Raymond Dietrich is held in high esteem. As a young man he founded LeBaron Carrossiers in New York City in partnership with Thomas Hibbard. Their first commission was for a custom seven-passenger limousine to be built by the Fleetwood Body Company over a

Packard chassis. Their reputation spread, and in 1922 the two-year-old LeBaron company was invited to exhibit at the New York Auto Salon. Edsel Ford placed an order for eight cars to be built on Lincoln chassis and eventually persuaded Dietrich to leave LeBaron and move to Detroit. Although he was the principal designer at LeBaron, the settlement arrangements did not allow Dietrich to take with him the special sweeps and curves—drawing templates he had made—that gave the LeBaron cars their distinctive style.[51]

Dietrich, Inc. of Detroit, began buying Packard chassis and creating custom bodies for financiers, industrialists, film producers and their stars, and leading sports figures. The Dietrich-styled Packards are now among the most prized of all classic cars.[52] Chassis by Lincoln, Pierce Arrow, Cadillac, Franklin and Duesenberg were also graced with Dietrich coachwork (fig. 104). Rudolph Valentino and Gloria Swanson were among

103.   A scene in a General Motors' styling studio in the 1940s. In the foreground is a large-scale model of a GM "torpedo" body with its slant-back rear window and trunk. In the rear are models of the "fish-tail" Cadillac of 1949. (*Courtesy General Motors Corporation.*)

104.  Raymond Dietrich. LeBaron 2-passenger coupé. 1935. (*Courtesy Raymond Dietrich.*)

his clients. The Lincoln Motor Car Company commissioned him to design and build a show car for the prestigious *Concours d'Elegance* in Paris. Dietrich created a sporty two-passenger convertible coupe with a rumble seat which won the top award, a gold medal. He was at the apex of a brilliant career creating elegant prestige cars for an exclusive audience when the Market Crash of 1929 decimated the ranks of paper millionaires. Dietrich, Incorporated, was absorbed by the Murray Body Company which continued to build bodies bearing the nameplate "Packard—Body by Dietrich." The designer himself became head of all exterior design at Chrysler.

Aerodynamic streamlining was not a consideration in Dietrich's design, but he did convey a sense of forward movement through a design line that rose quickly from the ground and arched over the front wheels, dropping back in a gentle reverse curve. The front fender had the approximate profile of the teardrop form (fig. 105), but the hoods were long and straight-lined. This suggested a powerful and massive engine, and the driver seemed in command of a formidable prow. Spare tires mounted in front-fender wells were reminiscent of the adventurous days of cross-country tours when provisions, fuel cans and spare parts were strapped

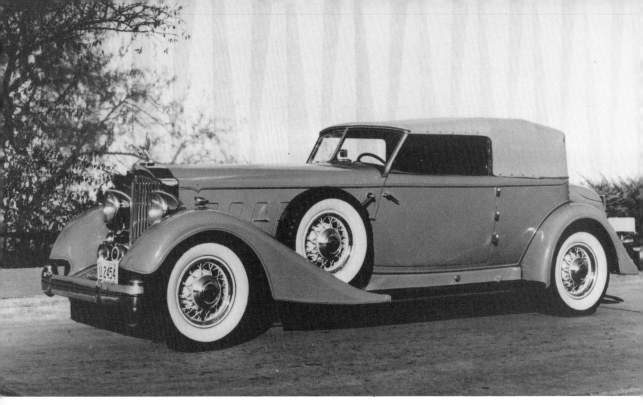

105.   Raymond Dietrich. *Packard Twelve* chassis with Dietrich Custom Victoria body. 1934. (*Courtesy Raymond Dietrich.*)

to the car. There was a "road-machine" look about certain classic cars that is now generally lost, along with the market for custom design.

For Dietrich line was everything, and his designs were marked by long graceful curves and clean, unbroken straight lines. The "line of least resistance" was simple and elegant. Typically, Dietrich sketched side elevations, and his classics were photographed from the side, views that devotees seem to prefer. Highly skilled coachbuilders knew how to develop three-dimensional form from these lines and were known to guard their own methods jealously.

There were probably few Americans who did not admire the classic cars for their marvelous engineering, their high degree of craftsmanship and their elegance of line. Those unable to appreciate such virtues might be impressed with the owners of such cars—the very rich, the very powerful and the very glamorous. Either way the classic cars represented the epitome of an earlier tradition of automobile design. The authority of this tradition tended to retard acceptance of fully streamlined cars.

## PRODUCTION CARS

The first problem of automobile manufacturers was the development of a durable reliable product. As demand increased, the emphasis shifted to production problems. Competition also increased, but there were few distinctive features in production cars; engineering progress narrowed the differences between competitive makes. A third phase began when stylists were called upon to create individuality through the autos' external appearances. The first American production car completely designed from headlight to rear bumper by a stylist appeared during the 1927 recession. A prominent West Coast stylist and custom-automobile builder, Harley J. Earl, had been commissioned by General Motors to design a new production automobile, the *La Salle,* for the Cadillac Motor Car Division. Earl incorporated some of the lines of custom cars on the smaller-scale *La Salle* (fig. 106) which was marketed as a lower-cost Cadillac. As a result of the new car's success, Earl remained at GM as head of a staff devoted to automotive appearance, the Art and Color Section.[53] As the title suggested, the work generally involved a surface treatment of color and trim applied to bodies already built by GM's Fisher Body Division. It also pointed up the attention being given to color as a factor in sales (see Chapter 3). Eventually, Earl and his staff developed a team approach with GM body engineers, and within ten years GM Styling was given general staff status. Earl's appointment as a vice-president in 1940 signaled the importance attributed to automobile appearance at the end of the decade.[54]

Because of the lead time necessary to work out details of body construction and to create tooling, the designer must create automobiles two or three years before their appearance in showrooms.[55] Raymond Loewy designed the 1934 *Hupmobile* sedan in 1932, simplifying its basic form by eliminating lines and excessive trim and blending forms together as much as practicable. His own design notations (fig. 107) outlined new

106.   Harley Earl. The 1927 *La Salle.* (*Courtesy General Motors Corporation.*)

*La Salle*

1927

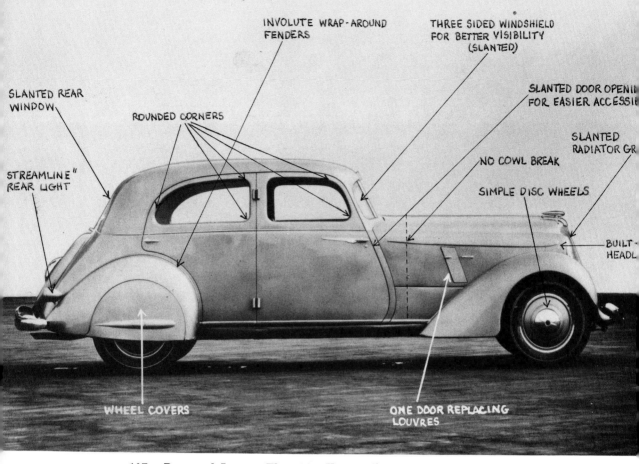

INVOLUTE WRAP-AROUND
FENDERS

THREE SIDED WINDSHIELD
FOR BETTER VISIBILITY
(SLANTED)

SLANTED DOOR OPENI
FOR EASIER ACCESSI

SLANTED REAR
WINDOW

ROUNDED CORNERS

SLANTED
RADIATOR GR

STREAMLINE"
REAR LIGHT

NO COWL BREAK

SIMPLE DISC WHEELS

BUILT-
HEADL

WHEEL COVERS

ONE DOOR REPLACING
LOUVRES

107. Raymond Loewy. The 1934 *Hupmobile*. (*Raymond Loewy/William Snaith, Inc.*)

trends that would become commonplace by the end of the decade. Loewy has always abided by his own MAYA (most advanced yet acceptable) principle for production design. However much a designer would like to advance his designs or elevate tastes, he must not outdistance public acceptance.

This may be what Chrysler did in creating the 1934 *Airflow* (fig. 108). It was a design based on scientific principles and extensive engineering tests. The result was the most streamlined American production automobile up to that time and so unconventional that a reviewer of the 1934 New York Automobile Show found it took two or three days to become accustomed to it.[56] The *Airflow* is said to have had its inception in 1927 when Carl Breer, chief engineer of the Chrysler Corporation, happened to observe the effortless, smooth flight of a flock of geese. Breer was surprised to find that the "geese" were in fact a V-formation of airplanes.[57] He reasoned that this application of organic forms could be made to automobiles as well as to aircraft. He sought advice from Orville Wright on the design of a wind tunnel, then had a test facility built at the Chrysler laboratories. Breer's original intent was to utilize the

phenomenon of lift in reverse in order to press the automobile more firmly against the highway at high speeds. This was to provide a steadier ride, but the goal was abandoned when it was determined that the pressing force would be negligible and that drag was a more serious problem.[58]

The teardrop form was ruled out for two reasons: first, it was felt that an extended tapered rear would be an impractical and vulnerable appendage in traffic and when parking. Secondly, the motor was to be located in the front with the driver in the center of the car; a teardrop form would restrict his vision. The chassis layout was not conventional, however. The rear seat was moved twenty inches forward from its traditional position over the rear axle. The engine was also moved forward to a position *between* the front wheels. These two innovations lowered vibration frequencies and eliminated the usual fore-and-aft pitching motion of traditional autos. A system of girders and beams formed the car's structure (fig. 109), with the passengers riding *inside* the frame rather than over it.

This arrangement for passenger comfort and safety thus established, wind-tunnel tests were run on hundreds of model bodies. Breer arrived at

109.  Frame construction of the *Airflow*. (*Courtesy Chrysler Corporation.*)

a form that resembled a section of an airplane wing with flat sides, a parabolic curve rising from the front bumper and dropping to the rear one. This form was then altered to accommodate a sloping windshield. Fenders and headlamps were partially absorbed into the body, and a slight upturn

110.  Interior, 1934 *Airflow.* (*Courtesy Chrysler Corporation.*)

and thinning of the trailing edges of front and rear fenders suggested the teardrop form. Interiors of the 1934 models were fitted out with marbled rubber floor mats, and relatively wide seats were framed in chrome tubing (fig. 110). Later models provided floor carpeting and fully upholstered seating as an alternative to the machine look. The two-piece slantback windshield could be opened for ventilation. (The Custom Imperial model had the first curved, one-piece windshield on an American production car.)

Advertisements for the first *Airflow* claimed the car was "functionally correct for cleaving through the air . . . and functionally correct for moving over the uneven surface of the ground," and promised "the greatest travel comfort man has ever enjoyed." [59] Ad men recognized that the interpretation of functionalism in 1934 had shifted from the static geometric forms promoted by the Bauhaus architects to the dynamic organic forms of nature:

> *Old mother nature has always designed her creatures for the function they are to perform. She has streamlined her fastest fish . . . her swiftest birds . . . her fleetest animals that move on land.*
>
> *You have only to look at a dolphin, a gull, or a greyhound to appreciate the rightness of the tapering, flowing contour of the new Airflow Chrysler.*
>
> *By scientific experiment, Chrysler engineers have simply verified and adapted a natural fundamental law.*[60]

The writer of this ad was likely unaware of Cayley's observations of trout and dolphins, Thompson's analysis of birds' wings and eggs or the full significance of Brancusi's abstracted seal, fish, birds and eggs, but he and his readers were sophisticated enough to grasp the analogy between natural and man-made streamlined forms. Other Chrysler ads promised "a glorious sense of freedom at high speeds" in the *Airflow,* a car "balanced like an arrow in flight." [61] References were made to wind-tunnel tests, but no specific claims of fuel savings or high speeds were made. The same virtues were implicit in the smaller but very similar DeSoto *Airflow.*

The Chrysler *Airflow* attracted 11,292 buyers in 1934, a figure that fell to 4,600 in its fourth and final year, 1937.[62] Henry Dreyfuss called the *Airflow*'s demise "the classic example of going too far too fast" with a design beyond public taste and acceptance.[63] There were other factors: the country underwent a recession beginning in August of 1937 which reached a low point the following March. Several industries, fearing inflated prices, had accumulated large inventories of materials. When finished products hit the market, there was insufficient purchasing power to absorb them, and workers were laid off, compounding the problem. The recovery from this began slowly in mid-1938 but Chrysler had already dropped what appeared to be its least promising product.

Raymond Dietrich feels the car failed to elicit a response from buyers (despite its claims) because it did not have a profile that implied forward motion. It should have risen quickly at the front and dropped off gradually at the rear, like the fenders of his custom cars. Although he had not developed the *Airflow*, as head of exterior design he altered the front grill in 1937 to give it a nearly vertical appearance and some sense of a sharp prow to cut through rather than "nose under" the air. If he was right, it may be that the *Airflow* was not too advanced but that it did not sufficiently resemble the teardrop the public had learned to identify as the ideal streamlined body. It would be incorrect to label the *Airflow* a failure, for it introduced several useful technical innovations, gave a high priority to passenger comfort and conditioned the public to accept partially streamlined cars before the end of the decade. A General Motors

111.   The 1934 *La Salle* 4-door sedan. (*Courtesy General Motors Corporation.*)

112.  The 1936 Lincoln *Zephyr*. (*Courtesy the Ford Archives, Dearborn, Michigan.*)

executive noted in 1939 that "streamlining has been the badge of up-to-dateness in all forms of industry, and we must continue with it and make the best of it." [64] The 1934 *LaSalle* (fig. 111) had already begun to adopt, with measured restraint, teardrop forms in its fenders, headlights and taillights. The General Motors "torpedo" bodies of 1940 made further use of absorption—merging fenders, headlights and hoods and further rounding the hood, roof and trunk line.

Similar moves were made at the Lincoln Division of the Ford Motor Company. The 1936 Lincoln *Zephyr* made extensive use of compound curves (fig. 112). The Lincoln *Continental* combined the sharp prow and recessed headlights of the *Zephyr* with a longer chassis, smooth planes and the trim appearance of Gordon Buehrig's *Cord 810* (fig. 113). Rear-wheel "pants," a distinctive spare-tire cover and fine interior and exterior craftsmanship added to the sense of fine quality (fig. 114). The *Continental* was based on sketches made in Europe by Edsel Ford and was intended as a custom model for his use. It attracted attention in Florida, and he persuaded his father to put the car into limited production in 1940. Public acceptance was high. In 1941 the Museum of Modern Art chose it as an example of excellence in product design.

European and American auto builders ignored the K-form in their prewar production models while Jaray's influence continued to be felt. The Czechoslovakian *Tatra* (fig. 115) followed Jaray's principles beginning with the 1934 *Type 77A*, a streamlined rear-engined car not unlike today's *Volkswagen*, but with a small vertical fin affixed to the rear.[65] At the time of German annexation in 1938, Tatra's designer and manager, Hans Ledwinka, was developing two rear-engine models, the *Type 87* (also

113.   Gordon Buehrig. The Cord *810*. 1936. (*Courtesy Chilton Publications and the Free Library of Philadelphia.*)

114.   Edsel Ford and Ford staff members. The Lincoln Continental. 1940. (*Courtesy the Ford Archives, Dearborn, Michigan.*)

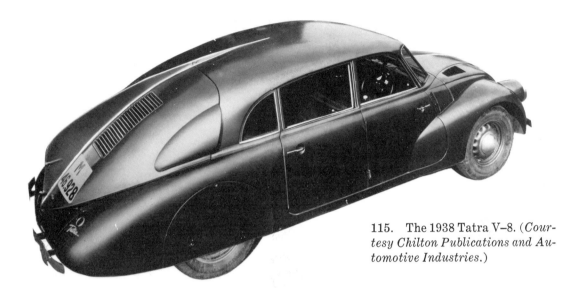

115. The 1938 Tatra V–8. (*Courtesy Chilton Publications and Automotive Industries.*)

116. Ferdinand Porsche. Prototypes of the 1937 (LEFT) and 1936 (RIGHT) Volkswagens. (*Courtesy Volkswagen of America, Inc.*)

117.   Count Alexis de Sakhnoffsky. Greyhound Motorcoach. *Ca.* 1937. Chassis and body were by the White and Bender Companies, respectively. (*Courtesy Motor Bus Society Collection.*)

with a small rear fin) and the *Type 97* which was put into production that year. In Germany, Dr. Ferdinand Porsche had since 1934 been developing a rear-engine *Kleinauto,* the inexpensive car Adolf Hitler wanted produced for the German working classes.[66] Three prototype *Volksautos* (as the German press called them) were tested in 1936 and later (fig. 116). The Führer ordered the formation of the Volkswagen Development Company in 1937, and the first thirty units, closely following Jaray's designs, were produced. The Nazis then forbade further production of the *Tatra Type 97* in Czechoslovakia, feeling it competed with the *Volkswagen.* Eventually, the Volkswagen Corporation, like the Chrysler Corporation, had to compensate for infringements upon the Jaray patents.

Two other kinds of road vehicles were modernized in the thirties. The Greyhound Corporation began to streamline its motor coaches, at first with a stylistic treatment of surface details that incorporated the look of the teardrop (fig. 117), and later by eliminating the forward hood and fenders, absorbing the engine and front wheels into a single large shell with rounded corners, the familiar "silversides" coach (fig. 118). At the same time the leaping greyhound logotype was enlarged, reinforcing the psychological nexus between nature's dynamic functionalism and man's desire for speed. In Los Angeles, Wally Byam began marketing a small two-wheel teardrop camping trailer, the *Airstream,* shown pulled by an *Airflow* on his business card with the inscription "the original torpedo

118.   Raymond Loewy. Greyhound "silversides" motorcoach. 1940. (*Courtesy Motor Bus Society Collection.*)

car." The parent company had marketed its self-contained *Road Yacht* as early as 1928, described as "a large metal bug on wheels" and providing a galley, tables, lavatory and sleeping accommodations for five. By 1936, the *Airstream Clipper* had assumed the rounded shell-form still seen on American highways.

As with the design of trains, streamlining has had a lasting effect on automobile designs, where it continues as "cleanlining"—an aesthetic of uncluttered forms and smooth surfaces. The experimental teardrop cars themselves never went into production but helped create a taste for lower, sleeker and better-designed cars. No doubt the public was torn between its fascination for the radically new teardrop, its respect for the elegant custom classics, and its love affair with the tin lizzie, the homely contraption that made driving available to so many. By the end of the decade, all three had become history, and a compromise had been reached in moderately streamlined cars in all price ranges.

# VII.
# ARCHITECTURE:
# THE STREAMLINED
# MODERNE

## ARCHITECTURE AND FLUID DYNAMICS

Even though buildings are stationary, the design of architectural structures must sometimes take into account fluid dynamics. Prevailing winds can challenge a building's stability as well as carry off the heat generated within. Dams and hydroelectric plants control the flow of water and must do so with minimal turbulence to avoid *cavitation* (a phenomenon associated with the rapid formation and collapse of vapor pockets), which has an abrasive effect on channel walls.

Buckminster Fuller has been preoccupied with problems of housing and structural design since the late 1920s. After a period of self-imposed solitude he concluded that a more comprehensive system—one acknowledging the whole of man's understanding of the universe—must be applied to housing, not only to satisfy practical needs but as a demonstration of man's mastery over his environment. To begin with, man must take a macroview of the problem, and Fuller generalized "home" to "shelter" to avoid traditional solutions. Furthermore, he determined that to ignore the potential of industrial methods, especially mass production,

128

was foolish for "anything that stands in the way of truth and TIME SAVING will ultimately perish." [1] He sketched an anecdote to show the folly of handcrafted homes: a man visits one of two thousand automobile designers, selects a period style, chooses thousands of parts from as many suppliers, arranges for a loan and leaves to the designer the business of sending out bids, selecting a builder and arranging for city building permits, inspections, etc. In the end, the auto takes six months to a year to build and costs $50,000. [2]

It seemed incredible to Fuller that, in the economic crisis of 1927, we had overlooked "the most essential product for industrial production— the home," and that perhaps now America was ready for "an honest-to-goodness twentieth century home," one that would be "functionally designed, dynamically balanced, and harmoniously presented." [3] He rejected the most ordinary method of construction, the piling of one mass upon

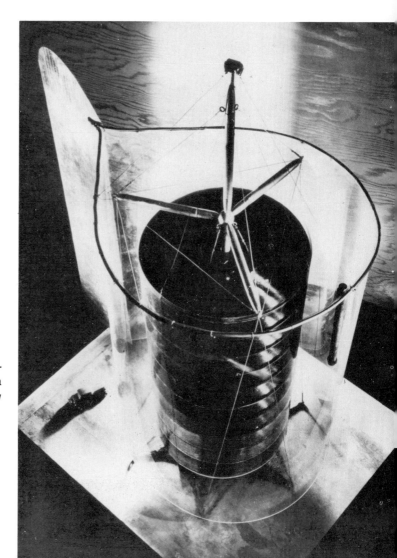

119.  Richard Buckminster Fuller. *4D* ten-deck structure with shield. 1927 and later. (*Courtesy R. Buckminster Fuller.*)

120.   Bureau of Reclamation. Hoover Dam. Dedicated in 1935. (*Courtesy Bureau of Reclamation, U.S. Dept. of the Interior.*)

another, in favor of lightweight metal structures. Compression would be balanced by tension as in the rigging of a sailboat, and with the parsimony of a true engineer he sought to accomplish the most with the least. His *Dymaxion 4D* house and his multiple-deck *4D* tower apartment were designed around a central mast, each deck supported by cables from the mast. They were to be light enough to be transported by dirigible, freeing them from the limitations of land-transported buildings; they could be delivered anywhere in the "air-ocean." [4]

One variation of the ten-deck structure incorporated a streamlined shield to reduce the heat losses associated with drag (fig. 119). He diagrammed the air currents for a cube, cylinder and streamlined form to show that a larger structure, if properly designed, would have no more wind resistance than a small structure without streamlining. The shield, a transparent streamform with an extended tail as a vane, would have been free to rotate, like a weathervane. One of the presumed advantages of the shield would be the reduction of the structural requirements needed to brace against the wind. With the mass of the building reduced, the air-delivery would be facilitated.

Applying aerodynamic principles to architecture was as logical to Fuller as applying them to automobiles.[5] In 1944 Fuller designed the *Dymaxion Dwelling Machine,* a home in which aerodynamic streamlining and modern technology were integrated. His intent was to produce housing on an assembly-line basis using aluminum and plastics. The floor plan was circular and the building was surmounted by a revolving ventilator that faced the wind. The vacuum created behind this device drew fresh air up through the home. Two prototypes of the *Dymaxion Dwelling Machine* were built at the Beech Aircraft plant in Wichita, Kansas. The technology of the air-frame industry was suited to the fabrication of the aluminum ribs, aprons and outer skin of the structures and provided the method of metal joining.[6]

Walter Dorwin Teague included a photograph of Hoover Dam in his book *Design this Day* as an example of "rightness of form." Construction on the project began in 1931; the last concrete was poured in 1935, and later that year President Roosevelt dedicated the dam (fig. 120). Behind the dam rise four intake towers, polygonal and stairstepped in Deco fash-

121.  A section through a spillway at Hoover Dam. (*Courtesy Bureau of Reclamation, U.S. Dept. of the Interior.*)

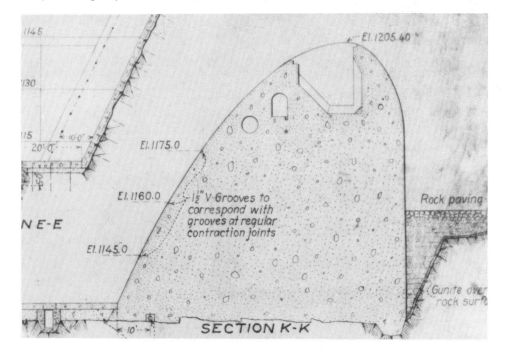

ion. The spillways on the Arizona and Nevada sides resemble aircraft wings with "engines." A section drawing of the spillway (fig. 121) resembles the vertical stabilizer of the *DC–3*. The similarity is not merely coincidental as both forms were developed from the same general principles.

Atop the dam on the Nevada side are two *Winged Figures of the Republic* (1940) created by Oskar J. W. Hansen. The streamlined figures are perched on a black diorite base and flank a flagpole and plaque dedicated to those who conceived and built the dam (fig. 122). Hansen explained the symbolism of the figures as follows:

> *The building of Hoover Dam belongs to the sagas of the daring. The winged bronzes which guard the flag therefore wear the look of eagles. To them was also given the vital upward thrust of an aspirational gesture; to symbolize the readiness for defense of our institutions and the keeping of our spiritual eagles ever ready....*[7]

## THE STREAMLINED MODERNE

Fuller's *Dymaxion* buildings and the Hoover Dam are streamlined but are not examples of the style now called the Streamlined Moderne. The Moderne is a variant of the International Style with much of that movement's starkness, severity and commitment to the processes and aesthetics of the machine age. But where the work of the Stijl and Bauhaus masters was uncompromising in its adherence to a canon of geometric functionalism, the Streamlined Moderne was less strident in voice, and its forms were relieved by organic lines. It was marked by a combination of flat and curved walls, light in tone and often topped with silvery handrails of tubular metal that enclosed terraces. Extensive use was made of glass blocks especially in the curved walls and around entranceways. Occasionally circular windows balanced rectangular elements. Aerodynamic principles were not applied to Streamlined Moderne buildings, but their curved roof lines and rounded corners provided the same smooth, continuous visual experience afforded by the *DC–3* and the *Hiawatha*. It is this experience that defines the significant forms of the period.

In 1931 Norman Bel Geddes projected a *House of Tomorrow* which anticipated and possibly inspired many Moderne houses of the decade. He felt that it would reverse many of the mistakes of recent housing, and

122. Oskar J. W. Hansen. *Winged Figures of the Republic.* 1940. (*Courtesy Bureau of Reclamation, U.S. Dept. of the Interior.*)

123.   Norman Bel Geddes. *The House of Tomorrow.* 1931. (*From the work of Norman Bel Geddes at the Hoblitzelle Theatre Arts Library, The Humanities Research Center, University of Texas, by permission of the executrix Edith Lutyens Bel Geddes.*)

he warned that its acceptance would require some jettisoning of old ideas and ideals. Clients would have to realign their priorities and have faith in progressive architects if improvements were to come, for

> *it must be realized that at the moment we are only on the threshold of what in a few years will undoubtedly be the universal architecture;*

124.   Norman Bel Geddes. Living Room, *House of Tomorrow.* (*From the work of Norman Bel Geddes at the Hoblitzelle Theatre Arts Library, The Humanities Research Center, University of Texas, by permission of the executrix Edith Lutyens Bel Geddes.*)

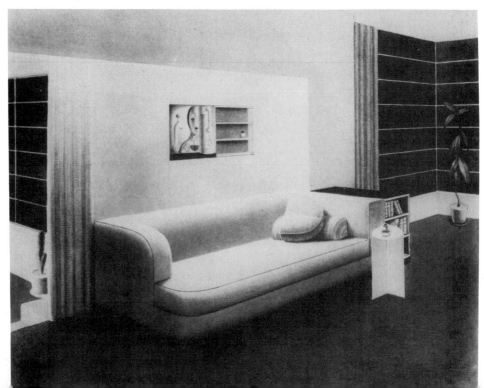

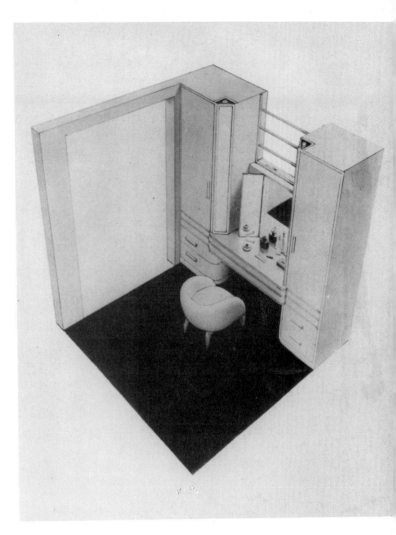

125.  Norman Bel Geddes. Wife's Dressing Room, *House of Tomorrow. (From the work of Norman Bel Geddes at the Hoblitzelle Theatre Arts Library, The Humanities Research Center, University of Texas, by permission of the executrix Edith Lutyens Bel Geddes.)*

*and to be able to visualize what that architecture will be like, the interested person must realize the principles which are governing those architects and designers who are trying to create what we may call the twentieth-century style.*[8]

Geddes's house was created in "the spirit of the age" and incorporated the open asymmetrical plan of Frank Lloyd Wright's *Robie House,* the neat detailing of the *Dessau Bauhaus* and Le Corbusier's fondness for roof terraces. Although the exterior featured a number of curvilinear elements (fig. 123), these were primarily roof lines; most of the rooms in the living area were rectangular. The large curved wall in front enclosed a two-car garage and the living room faced the gardens behind the home.[9] This reversed the layout of American bungalows of the twenties. The interior walls were to be free of moldings and cornices, because "the over-ornamentation and elaboration of the past" were no longer suited to modern "forthright" people.[10] One should expect the interior to fulfill the promise of the exterior: simplicity, freedom from intricate decoration and

126.   Frank Lloyd Wright. Johnson's Wax Administration Building, Racine, Wisconsin. 1937–39. (*Courtesy Johnson's Wax.*)

reliance upon the beauty of form.[11] In the living room, the severe rectangularity would be relieved by the swelling curves of an overstuffed sofa, by works of art and by potted plants (fig. 124). Spacious windows would admit health-giving sunlight and offer a generous view of the private garden. On the second level, Geddes provided the lady of the house a dressing room (fig. 125) with a built-in vanity and indirect lighting.[12] His restraint was admirable. An Art Deco designer might have embellished the cabinets with harlequins, sunrays or fountains and edged them with faceted stair-stepped moldings; Geddes simply rounded the edges and added three horizontal accents.[13] He favored the "mirror-like brilliance" of stainless steel. With its rounded corners, flush doors and built-in appliances, the kitchen was "streamlined" both in appearance and in its efficient and logical arrangement.[14] Although many features of the house echoed ideas seen at Le Corbusier's *L'Esprit Nouveau* Pavillion at the 1925 Paris Exposition, Geddes helped to popularize new trends by reaching, through the *Ladies' Home Journal,* American audiences unable to visit traveling exhibits and unfamiliar with architectural journals.

Not all architecture with curved walls can be classified as Streamlined Moderne, which was a style that led to superficial applications. It is worth noting that Frank Lloyd Wright demonstrated the breadth of his powers during the 1930s by creating two totally dissimilar buildings. The Johnson's Wax Company Administration Building (fig. 126) and the Kaufmann House ("Falling Water") date from the same period. The latter is a series of cantilevered rectangular masses, while in the former, curved masses merge one into the other, suggesting organic references. Devoid of windows, the exterior appears self-contained, a shell-like form with its

127.   Interior, Johnson's Wax Administration Building. (*Courtesy Johnson's Wax.*)

128.   An executive office in the Johnson's Wax Administration Building. (*Courtesy Johnson's Wax.*)

entrances hidden in recesses. Inside (fig. 127) the horizontal accents recall the wrap-around bands that had become a hallmark of streamlined products. Circular tubes of Pyrex diffuse the light, softening the interior visually as the curved walls had softened the exterior. Wright also designed the furniture in the office area. The desks have rounded "drawer" units that swing out on one side and an oval top (fig. 128). Officially opened at the same time as the 1939 New York World's Fair, the Johnson's Wax Building was described by *Life* magazine as possibly "a truer glimpse of the shape of things to come" than the Fair's *World of Tomorrow*.

The Streamlined Moderne was easily identified as an "up-to-date" style, and it proved useful to corporations wishing to project a new image. The Walgreen Drug Company built a number of Moderne stores before and after the Second World War. Its store in Miami (fig. 129) is a series of glass and cement layers that curve around two sides, stepping inward at the corner to emphasize the rounded main entrance. The modest neon electrographics repeat the horizontal lines and are confined mainly to this area.

Kem Weber was a leading practitioner of the Moderne in California, designing stores, homes, furnishings and movie sets. For a proposed remodeling of the Sommer and Kaufmann shoe store in San Francisco (fig. 130), he envisioned wraparound display windows with semicircular corners. Raymond Loewy and Lee Simonson used similar forms in their design

129. Ralph Zimmerman (*Zimmerman, Saks and McBride, Chicago.*) Walgreen Drug Store, Miami, Florida. 1937. (*Courtesy the Walgreen Company.*)

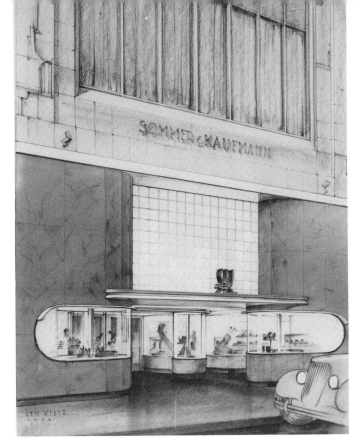

130. Kem Weber. Proposed re-modeling, Sommer and Kaufmann shoe store, San Francisco. 1936. (*Original drawing from the Kem Weber Architectural Collection of the Art Galleries, University of California, Santa Barbara, and first published in Kem Weber: The Moderne in Southern California by David Gebhard and Harriette Von Breton [1969].*)

131. Raymond Loewy and Lee Simonson. Corner of an Industrial Designer's office and studio. 1934. (*Raymond Loewy/William Snaith, Inc.*)

of a model industrial designer's office and studio (fig. 131). Installed in the Contemporary American Industrial Arts Exposition of 1934 at the Metropolitan Museum of Art, New York, the walls were of ivory Formica, the floor was cadet blue linoleum and the furniture was of yellow leather and gun metal blue tubing. Walter Dorwin Teague designed an equally trim Moderne interior for the lounge of the Ford Exposition at the 1939 New York World's Fair (fig. 132). Like the functional designs of Weber and Loewy, Teague's interior was free of the cliché motifs of the Art Deco period.

132.   Walter Dorwin Teague. Lounge interior, Ford Exposition, New York World's Fair. 1939. (*Walter Dorwin Teague Associates, Inc.*)

133. Norman Bel Geddes. "Skyscraper" cocktail shaker and "Manhattan" serving tray. 1937. (*Courtesy Revere Copper and Brass Company.*)

## FURNISHING THE MODERNE HOME

Small products and appliances were among the first goods restyled after the 1927 recession. For these the cost of retooling was less than for automobiles, and marketing new styles was less of a financial risk. Moreover, the new styles imported to America after the 1925 Paris exposition took the form of fabrics, furniture and such decorative arts as silver, china, candelabra, lamps and jewelry. Because of the wide range of Art Deco motifs and the introduction of new forms inspired by streamlined transport designs, some manufacturers began to offer a variety of products. The Revere Copper and Brass Company, for example, included in their 1937 gift catalogue items in floral, geometric, streamlined and novelty styles. Customers preferring the symbolism of the twenties might choose the "skyscraper" cocktail shaker and the "Manhattan" tray with its stairstepped rim, both by Norman Bel Geddes (fig. 133). For those more attuned to the newer organic forms, Revere offered a polished chromium "Normandie" water pitcher by Peter Mueller-Munk, said to be "inspired by the streamlined stacks of the famous French liner" (fig. 134).

Household appliances that had been treated simply as machines

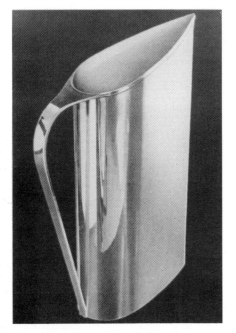

134. Peter Mueller-Monk. Normandie water pitcher. 1937. (*Courtesy Revere Copper and Brass Company.*)

135. The Hoover *Model 150* Vacuum. 1936. (*Courtesy The Hoover Company.*)

were now styled to match the Moderne domestic environment and to signify, by their new casing, improvements in design and performance. Hoover's *Model 105* vacuum of 1920 resembled the work of the German designer-architect Peter Behrens, whose appliances made a virtue of exposed screws and assemblies of simple but disparate components. By 1936, the Hoover had assumed the new symbolism (fig. 135). Its teardrop motor-housing gave the vacuum a lower, sleeker appearance and the total effect was more harmonious. Sharp edges and screws that might scratch furniture were eliminated. Whether such redesigns created demands or satisfied them is debatable. In any event, they made products more saleable.

The basic principle of streamlining in transport design had been to blend subforms into harmonious organic whole forms with transitional curves. Protuberances, seams and gaps were eliminated because they induced surface drag. These same principles were applied to stationary forms of the thirties for aesthetic reasons and for practical ones. Such forms were easier to clean and grasp and presented fewer hazards than those with cracks, squared corners and sharp edges. Buckminster Fuller "streamlined" his *Dymaxion* bathroom for these reasons.

The bathroom was originally designed for Fuller's *4D* house of 1927. In 1930, the first prototype was constructed in the Detroit engineer-

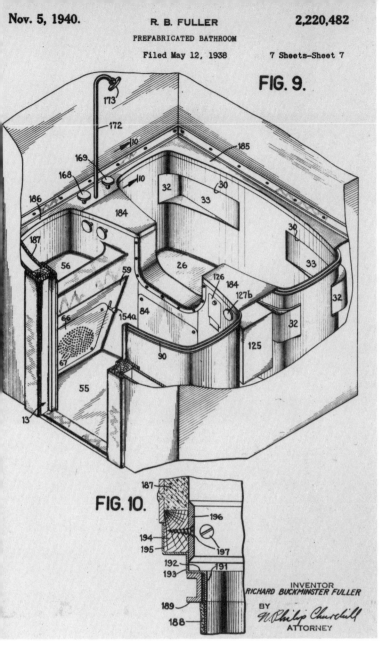

Nov. 5, 1940.

R. B. FULLER

2,220,482

PREFABRICATED BATHROOM

Filed May 12, 1938

7 Sheets-Sheet 7

FIG. 9.

FIG. 10.

INVENTOR
RICHARD BUCKMINSTER FULLER
BY
N. Philip Churchill
ATTORNEY

136. Richard Buckminster Fuller. Patent drawing for *Dymaxion* bathroom. 1938. (*Courtesy R. Buckminster Fuller.*)

ing laboratories of William Stout, designer of the Pullman *Railplane* and the Stout *Scarab* automobile. The prototype was not shown to the public because the sponsor, the American Radiator Company, feared the reaction of plumbers' unions. The Phelps Dodge Corporation had a dozen units built in 1936 but the design was never put into full production.[15] The prefabricated unit consisted of two compartments, one for the tub-shower and another for a washbowl and a water closet (fig. 136). Numerous features made the unit convenient, hygienic and safe. Prototypes were of plated copper, but Fuller foresaw their ultimate fabrication in plastics. Prefabricated showers and tubs of fiberglass have since become a reality.

A wide variety of household goods were streamlined during the

137.  W. Archibald Welden. Revere Ware. 1939. (*Courtesy Revere Copper and Brass Company.*)

138.  The Maytag *Model 90* Washing Machine. 1927. (*Courtesy The Maytag Company.*)

139.  The Maytag *Model 10* Washing Machine. 1933. (*Courtesy The Maytag Company.*)

140. The Singer Sewing Machine. 1939. (*Courtesy The Singer Company.*)

141. The Automatic Electric *Monophone.* 1928. (*Courtesy GTE Automatic Electric.*)

thirties. Some continue, like the line of Revere Ware that made its appearance in 1939 (fig. 137), to look modern and perform admirably. Over one hundred million pieces of Revere Ware have been produced; the soundness of their design and fabrication assure their position in the marketplace. Streamlining improved the visual appeal of the Maytag washing machine which had an "institutional" look in 1927 (fig. 138) but which, by 1933 began to respond to consumer demands for more attractive appliances (fig. 139). Sewing machines, nearly a necessity in a Depression economy, came to resemble modern furniture (fig. 140), a far cry from their origins as cast iron machinery.

Few products undergo such thorough and continuing reevaluation as the telephone. The cradle phone had the advantage (over the "candlestick" model) of freeing one hand. It was streamlined (fig. 141) in the sense of acquiring a simplified organic form suited to the human hand. Once an interest in streamlined forms developed, even durable and reliable products like the "monitor top" refrigerator (fig. 142) were replaced by newer models with concealed mechanisms (fig. 143). Raymond Loewy pioneered the type with Sears' *Coldspot* refrigerators in 1935, forcing other manufacturers to update their own models. Console model radios and television receivers were extended to the floor (fig. 144) like refrigerators and stoves, suggesting solidity and some reduction in floor cleaning.

Occasionally new products of the decade exhibited a sense of lightness, like Kem Weber's easily assembled *Airline Chair* (fig. 145) or

Teague's Steinway piano. The chromed tubing and thin wood members of the latter reduced both its physical and "visual" weight. Metal and glass tables were even more weightless in appearance (fig. 146) and had the hard and gleaming appearance that suited the machine style.

## THE ARCHITECTURE OF FANTASY

The more dramatic examples of the Streamlined Moderne, especially the temporary architecture of the 1939 New York World's Fair, were often sculptural. Their plasticity suggests historical precedents other than the International Style. The early work of Eric Mendelsohn was both monumental and dynamic. The plasticity of his *Einstein Tower* (fig. 147), completed in 1921, evolved from considerations of the projected media, poured concrete. Continuous lines flowed around the structure, giving it an organic quality not unlike Brancusi's sculpture.[16] Although its function as an observatory called for a vertical structure, the thrust of the form suggested horizontal movement behind which the main staircase seemed to trail.[17] The sweeping taper of the staircase echoed the (essentially)

142. The General Electric *Model T-7* Refrigerator. Manufactured from 1927 to 1938. (*Courtesy General Electric.*)

143. The General Electric *Model V-7* Refrigerator. 1936. (*Courtesy General Electric.*)

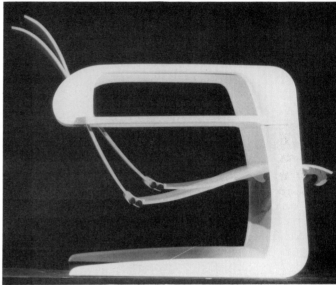

144. The RCA Victor *Model TRK-9* Television Receiver. 1939. (*Courtesy RCA.*)

146. Walter Dorwin Teague. Grand Piano for Steinway and Sons. 1939. (*Walter Dorwin Teague Associates, Inc.*)

teardrop-shaped windows of the entrance foyer. This dynamic quality is seen in other projects of this period with which Mendelsohn was occupied: automobile factories, film studios and railway stations—all connected with the idea of movement.

The *Einstein Tower* belongs stylistically with a series of sketches Mendelsohn began in 1914. One in particular, a proposed optical factory of 1917, appears to be the direct predecessor of the observatory, with its repetition of masses, heavy "buttresses" and horizontal layers of curved glass windows. Aldous Huxley saw Mendelsohn's "streamlined towers . . . [with] their insistent striation—stripe above horizontal stripe—of iron and glass" as spectacular examples of architectural romanticism.[18]

With the attention enjoyed by the *Normandie*, the *Nieuw Amsterdam* and other luxury liners, it was perhaps inevitable that the nautical metaphor would be combined with the Streamlined Moderne. One result was the *Aquatic Park Casino* (now the Maritime Museum) in San Francisco. Under the sponsorship of the city fathers, the Works Projects Administration began, in 1935, construction of a park at the foot of Van Ness Avenue. Flanking the central structure were bleachers facing the Bay, intended for viewing aquatic contests and pageants. The grounds were

147. Eric Mendelsohn. The Einstein Tower, Potsdam. 1921. (*Courtesy Mrs. Eric Mendelsohn.*)

148.   William Mooser, Jr. The Aquatic Park Casino (now the Maritime Museum),
San Francisco. 1935–39. (*Author's Collection.*)

dotted with granite seals, penguins and frogs by sculptor Beniamino Bu-
fano. These streamlined mammals extended the marine motif to the 1,800-
foot promenade that bordered the bathing beach.

At the center of the promenade stood the *Casino* (fig. 148), designed by William Mooser, Jr., then San Francisco head of the WPA.[19]
The Administration's press releases described the Casino as "streamlined
and modern to the last degree. . . . With rounded ends, set-back upper
stories, porthole windows and ship rails, its resemblance to a luxurious
ocean liner is indeed startling." [20] The effect was more pronounced before awnings and shrubbery were added. The interior of the four-level
*Casino* was decorated by Hilaire Hiler and his colleagues from the Federal
Art Project, Sargent Johnson, Richard Ayer and Robert Clark. Among
their motifs were flowing arabesques symbolizing ocean waves, references
to the lost continent of Atlantis, various marine plants and animals, and
a Polynesian sea-god, all "rich in symbolic as well as biological significance." Flanking the portico were terra-cotta sea deities. In some rooms
real rope was embedded in the plaster and the walls were festooned with
flags of the various western yacht clubs.

The Park was formally opened early in 1939; within three years
the *Casino* was padlocked. Its restaurant had gone bankrupt for lack of

149. Robert Derran. The Coca-Cola Bottling Plant, Los Angeles. Remodeling begun in 1937. (*Courtesy Coca-Cola Bottling Company of Los Angeles.*)

business. The frigid waters of the Bay discouraged most bathers and the tides had carried off much of the beach's imported sand.[21] What was worse, the Department of Health decreed that nearby sewerage effluence made the waters of the lagoon unsafe for bathing. After twelve years, the *Casino* was converted to a museum. Its nautical Moderne form is appropriate for a repository of figureheads, anchors, ships' models and documents related to the city's maritime history.

Another landlocked Moderne structure sits in downtown Los Angeles. In 1937 the principals of the Coca-Cola Bottling Company of Los Angeles decided to remodel their three Spanish-style office buildings and to combine them in one facade. Architect Robert Derran spared no nautical motifs on the building, which is replete with portholes, catwalks, hatches and a flying bridge splendid enough for any captain of industry (fig. 149). The building is awash in marine metaphors and, like her sister ship at Aquatic Park, she is topped by a mast. Wall surfaces and doorframes are treated to resemble riveted steel. At the "stern," a gigantic stucco Coke bottle reaffirms the true nature and purpose of the "ship." [22] As an outstanding example of the architecture of fantasy, the Coca-Cola building is natural to the City of Angels, where, as Reyner Banham tells us, architecture is in the public domain and deals in symbolic meanings all Angelenos can read.[23]

Kathleen Church Plummer has traced some of the roots of the Streamlined Moderne to science-fiction magazines and to the utopian visions of H. G. Wells.[24] The futuristic cities that were painted for *Amazing Stories* and other "pulps" variously anticipate or reflect the advanced designs of Buckminster Fuller, Norman Bel Geddes and other pioneering designers of the thirties. A central image in the Wellsian vision was a city of the future with "titanic buildings, curving spaciously in either direction," and roofed over with glass to create an enclosed, artificial environment.[25] In Wells's 1936 film version of *Things to Come,* montage photography combined live actors with fantastic Moderne model sets (fig. 150). A contemporary writer described the illusion created:

> *Deep in sunless caverns a new society, clad in garments containing complete radio telephone systems, inhabits windowless buildings,*

150. Vincent Korda. Model set for *Things to Come.* 1936. (*The Museum of Modern Art/Film Stills Archives.*)

151. Frank Lloyd Wright. Interior, Johnson's Wax Administration Building, Racine. (*Courtesy Johnson's Wax.*)

> *strolls along avenues from which automobiles are conspicuously absent and stands on broad flights of anachronistic steps. Communication seems to be largely by means of suspended railways, and elevators, mysteriously rising and descending in mammoth tubes of glass, give access to the different levels.*[26]

Wright created a self-contained environment in the Johnson's Wax offices the following year, providing the workers with natural foliage and sunlight (fig. 151). Norman Bel Geddes's ocean liner, airliner, train and motor coach, with their air-conditioning and internal food, sanitation and entertainment systems, provided similar insulation from bad weather, engine noise and other unpleasantries. In a sense, these closed environ-

152. Philip Nowland and Dick Caulkins. Futuristic city from *Buck Rogers*. Early 1930s. (*Permission granted by Robert C. Dille.*)

ments provided psychic insulation from the sight of bread lines, riots and the streets of Hooverville.[27]

Another source for the Streamlined Moderne was the comic strip. Philip Nowland and Dick Caulkins began *Buck Rogers* in 1930; Alex Raymond's *Flash Gordon* appeared four years later. The cities portrayed in *Buck Rogers* tended to the eclectic and ornamental (fig. 152). Those in *Flash Gordon* were sleeker and more curvilinear. The gadgetry in *Buck Rogers* provided the occasion for adventures in which personal mobility nearly becomes an end in itself (fig. 153).[28] Although the earlier sequences in the strip show teardrop-shaped spaceships, the space hardware of later adventures became more varied and fanciful. In these finny, ornate contraptions, one senses the inspiration for the *supersonic* streamlined automobiles of the 1950s.

153. Philip Nowland and Dick Caulkins. Space hardware from *Buck Rogers*. Mid-1930s. (*Permission granted by Robert C. Dille.*)

CAPTAIN BUCK ROGERS
leading
**Earth's Battle Fleet**

*roared across the vast void of the planetary space to engage in combat the powerful space ships of the marauding—*

**TIGER MEN**
OF
**MARS!**

Go with **BUCK ROGERS** Into Amazing New Worlds!

# VIII.
# THE WORLD OF TOMORROW

## THE APOTHEOSIS OF THE DESIGNERS

The reputations of Geddes, Dreyfuss, Teague and Loewy grew steadily during the decade as each added new clients and unveiled their latest design innovations. They were given their greatest challenge and opportunity when their talents were recruited for the 1939 New York World's Fair. The theme of the Fair—"Building the World of Tomorrow"—provided a perfect vehicle for their imaginations. They conjured up an optimistic preview of a future America where the advances of science, the capability of technology and the wisdom of good design would shape an orderly, healthy and content society. The vision materialized in symbolic architecture, models and dioramas, murals and multimedia pageants, all in graphic terms the public could grasp. Grover Whalen, president of the corporation that produced the Fair, had promised it would have value for the man on the street, for it would "attempt to bring into focus for his benefit the interplay of terrestrial elements and forces so that, realizing their possibilities under proper direction, he may plan a better existence." [1]

The Fair's exhibits were grouped by function. In addition to the amusement and recreation areas, the foreign exhibit area and a government zone, there were three major thematic zones. The first was devoted to transportation, communication, production, distribution and business administration. The second dealt with advances in shelter, sustenance and clothing. The third was reserved for education, religion, health, recreation and the arts. For each major zone there was a "key" exhibit to dramatize the major ideas in that area. The key exhibits were surrounded and supported by commercial displays that continued the theme of the zone.

The dominant symbol of the Fair was the Theme Center—two adjoining structures: a 700-foot obelisk called the *Trylon* and a 200-foot-diameter *Perisphere* (fig. 154).[2] Etched though they may be in the minds of those who visited the Fair or who saw one of the many thousand photographs of them in newspapers and magazines, these two gigantic, pristine geometric solids were like most Fair architecture, quite temporary. The transitory nature of the buildings, things of wood and wire and stucco, released the designers from the oppression of designing for posterity.

Visitors entered the Perisphere and proceeded to one of two ring-shaped balconies suspended over a miniature city—*Democracity*—"symbol of a perfectly integrated, futuristic metropolis pulsing with life and rhythm and music."[3] As the balconies rotated slowly, lights were dimmed to suggest dusk. Evening stars began to twinkle in the dome above as the room darkened. Symphonic music and a great chorus were heard as men of various occupations approached (fig. 155), projected onto the dome from movie projectors hidden around the balconies. These men, a narrator explained, represented the varied elements of society whose cooperation would provide the better life of leisure in the happiness that would be enjoyed in *Democracity*. The model city and the production were designed by Henry Dreyfuss, following the typical themes of world's fairs: progress and brotherhood. One is reminded of Prince Albert's comments about the first world's fair, held in the Crystal Palace in London in 1851:

> *None will doubt that we are living in a most remarkable period of transition, laboring forcefully toward that great aim indicated everywhere by history: the union of the human race. . . . Gentlemen, the exhibition of 1851 shall give a vivid picture of the stage at which humanity has arrived in the solution of that great task.*[4]

Raymond Loewy was responsible for the Focal Exhibit for the Transportation Zone, located in the Chrysler Motors Building—an ovoid hall adjoining a rectangular showroom and flanked by two Moderne towers

155. Henry Dreyfuss. Finale of the *Democracity* presentation inside the *Perisphere*. 1939. (*From the Henry Dreyfuss Archive, Cooper-Hewitt Museum of Decorative Arts and Design, Smithsonian Institution.*)

154. An overview of the 1939 New York World's Fair showing the *Trylon* and *Perisphere* in the middle ground and the Transportation Zone in the foreground, including the General Motors Building in the center, Ford's spiral *Road of Tomorrow* to the right and the Chrysler Motors Building at the lower right. (*Courtesy General Motors Corporation.*)

156. Raymond Loewy. The Chrysler Motors Building, 1939 New York World's Fair. (*Raymond Loewy/William Snaith, Inc.*)

(fig. 156). Above its central doorway a 38-foot animated mural constantly changed colors. A novel feature of the showrooms was the *Frozen Forest* where Airtemp refrigeration equipment created a frosted coating on artificial trees. Loewy was also consulting designer for the Railroad Building which housed three exhibits. Under its eight-story dome was housed a cyclorama designed by Leonard Outhwaite. Here animated models demonstrated the construction of railroads, the mining and smelting of ore, and the cutting and processing of timber. In a second area, Loewy's display of animated dioramas showed the services rendered to the public by American railroads. An adjoining auditorium housed an operating model railroad designed by Paul Penhune. Outside, Loewy's latest design for the Pennsylvania Railroad, the *S-1* engine, ran on its treadmill, functioning at an equivalent to sixty miles per hour. In a nearby outdoor amphitheater, four thousand spectators enjoyed the "Railroads on Parade" pageant staged by Edward Hungerford. With narration, orchestra music and a chorus of 250 actors and dancers in costumes of various eras, the pageant dramatized the romance of American transport. The real "stars" were the engines and cars that rolled across the stage, beginning with wood-burning steam engines and completing the story with modern streamlined diesel trains.[5] The Railroad Building was decorated with five murals by Griffith Baily Coale, some of which showed idealized male nudes holding streamlined engines and cars. The figures resembled the trains, having the sleek, glossy appearance of metal.

Walter Dorwin Teague and his associates counted among their World's Fair clients the A. B. Dick Company, National Cash Register, Consolidated Edison, Dupont, Kodak and Ford. The Electric Company's exhibit included a diorama of model skyscrapers illuminated from within and titled *The City of Light*. The National Cash Register Building was crowned by a gigantic "cash register" that rang up daily Fair attendance figures. At the Ford exhibit, visitors could test-drive a new automobile along the *Road of Tomorrow*, a half-mile elevated concourse that wound around and through the exhibit hall and down a spiral ramp. In addition to his role as a major designer of exhibits, Teague served on the Board of Design where he pressed for and succeeded in getting a change in the theme.[6] Others wished to commemorate a series of events from American history. Teague preferred to look forward rather than backward and insisted that the future would better serve as the unifying theme. His preference was characteristic to his profession, for the new designers had been promoting the reshaping of objects and the reordering of cities, institutions and priorities.

Despite their dependence upon manufacturing and business, the industrial designers had an idealistic sense of purpose. Teague's victory in redirecting the theme gave them the opportunities to present their ideas to millions of people. For their audience they sometimes found it necessary to make ideas graphic and simple to grasp. They knew that great throngs of people had to be moved through exhibit halls in a relatively short time and that many viewers would already have seen numerous other displays. For this reason complexities and nuances were rejected in favor of clear symbols and generalities. They both delighted and instructed, and in the process they and the profession of industrial design became even better known and admired. Press releases portrayed them in glowing terms, giving rise to the notion that the industrial designer was a Leonardo reborn, an artist-engineer with a probing mind and great foresight. In truth, the designers were dependent upon their staffs, but they personified a new enthusiasm and boldness that would energetically attack problems of any size and nature.

## FUTURAMA

Along with Dreyfuss, Loewy and Teague, other designers—including Donald Desky, Gilbert Rohde, Russel Wright, Morris Lapidus and Egmont Arens—created commercial exhibits for the World's Fair. The most extensive and comprehensive vision of the future, however, was provided by Norman Bel Geddes. His Highways and Horizons building for General

157.   A cutaway view of the Highways and Horizons Exhibit. The *Futurama* exhibit, "a vast cross-section of America in dramatic terms of 1960," occupied two levels in the foreground. (*Courtesy General Motors Corporation.*)

158.   Norman Bel Geddes and Albert Kahn. The General Motors Highways and Horizons Exhibit, 1939 New York World's Fair. (*Courtesy General Motors Corporation.*)

Motors occupied a full city block in area and proved to be the most popular exhibit at the Fair.[7] Actually a complex of buildings which Geddes assembled within a single exterior shell (fig. 157), the Highways and Horizons exhibit provided entertaining and educational displays and demonstrations in its showrooms and theater. Those entering the main entrance passed by the latest streamlined engine, a 4,000-hp. Electro-Motive diesel. Most preferred to begin with the more spectacular *Futurama* display. Long ramps led them to an upper level of the structure (fig. 158). Once inside, they stepped onto a moving sidewalk, and from this they were seated in one of several hundred comfortable upholstered chairs moving along a conveyor at the same speed as the sidewalk. Two visitors shared a compartment that had loudspeakers mounted inside its walls. A recorded narration, synchronized with the movement, welcomed them to a "magic Aladdin-like flight through time and space," and explained that the *Futurama* was not designed as a projection of any particular highway or program, but rather "to demonstrate in dramatic fashion that the world, far from being finished, is hardly yet begun; that the job of building the future is one which will demand our best energies, our most fruitful imagination; and that with it will come greater opportunities for all."[8]

As their compartments entered the *Futurama*, the visitors saw, spread below them, a panorama that covered 35,738 square feet and contained a million scaled-down trees and a half-million model buildings.[9] Along the superhighways, the special feature of the exhibit, traveled 50,000 teardrop cars, trucks and buses. *Futurama* demonstrated how this great motorway system would someday link city with countryside and residential, commercial and industrial centers with resorts. What has since become commonplace provided a preview of the world of 1960: nonstop elevated expressways with traffic separated according to speed and on-and-off ramps connecting with older roads (fig. 159). Geddes also forecast speeds of up to 100 miles per hour, traffic control bridges that would radio instructions to drivers, and highway surfaces illuminated by tubular lights in the safety curbs.

During their sixteen-minute tour, the visitors viewed "as though from a low-flying aircraft" mountains, valleys, lakes and streams, villages, towns and cities, industrial and university centers as they might look in two decades. Geddes even built a miniature, hygienic dairy farm and experimental farms (fig. 160) where fruit trees were protected by glass domes. ("Strange? Fantastic? Unbelievable? Remember this is the world of 1960!") Farther along the superhighway was a prosperous steel town and a modern university where "the youth of 1960 study for and envision their future in a world of still greater progress and achievement."[10] At a moun-

159. A workman prods a balky scale-model teardrop car on a *Futurama* superhighway. (*Courtesy General Motors Corporation.*)

160. An experimental farm of the future (1960) in the *Futurama* exhibit. (*Courtesy General Motors Corporation.*)

tain vacation paradise, viewers were reminded that high-speed autos and safe superhighways could make remote pleasures available even on limited vacation schedules. Finally the highway crossed over a suspension bridge and entered a gigantic metropolis (fig. 161):

> *Modern and efficient city-planning—breath-taking architecture— each city block a complete unit in itself. Broad, one-way thorough- fares—space, sunshine, light and air.*[11]

The city's concrete-and-glass towers were in the Moderne style with rounded corners and rooftop terraces. Geddes provided one-way streets for his teardrop autos and elevated pedestrian walkways (fig. 162). At the end of the *Futurama* ride, visitors returned to the outdoors and a full-scale intersection formed by the four buildings in the General Motors complex (fig. 163).

The *Futurama* exhibit showed that by the end of the decade Geddes had shifted his attention from problems of individual components—vehicles and buildings—to entire systems—superhighways, grand-scale urban plans and the relation of technology to the landscape. Streamlining was now applied in the broadest sense to these systems because "a free-flowing movement of people and goods across our nation is a requirement of modern living and prosperity." [12] He summed up his views on highway design in his second book, *Magic Motorways* (1940), illustrated with photographs of the *Futurama* exhibit, which he said had given five million visitors "a dramatic and graphic solution" to the "planless, suicidal mess" of the highways of today.[13] The diorama had demonstrated that an efficient motorway system could be laid down with the principles of safety, comfort, speed and economy. "One of the best ways to make a solution understandable to everyone," he wrote, "is to make it visual, to dramatize it." [14]

161.   A metropolis of tomorrow in the *Futurama* exhibit. (*Courtesy General Motors Corporation.*)

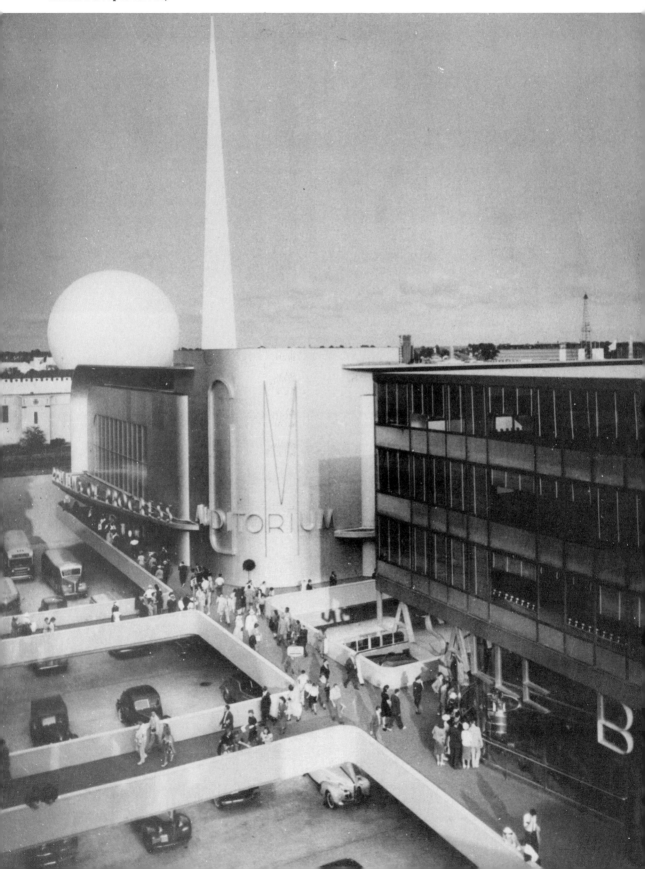

163. The full-scale intersection at the Highways and Horizons. (*Courtesy General Motors Corporation.*)

## BEYOND TOMORROW

If the 1960 world of *Futurama* seemed somewhat distant to fair-goers, parts of the Focal Exhibit of the Transportation Zone must have appeared as remote as the society of Wells's *Things to Come*. In it Loewy combined projected movies, animated maps and scale models. The film presentation was in three parts: the early period of transportation on foot, on animal and by chariot and Viking ship; the middle period, in which visitors saw American covered wagons, the pony express and the clipper ships; and finally, the mechanical period. In the latter the film showed "the swift automobile, the stream-lined train, the Zeppelin, and the modern plane that can encircle the globe—25,000 miles—in less than one week." [15]

Below the projection area was the *Rocketport of the Future,* a model of an enormous cannon barrel supported by massive buttressing, a machine so great that it dwarfed the ocean liners at the model docks around it (fig. 164). The *Rocketport* provided the show's spectacular finale. When

164. Raymond Loewy. The *Rocketport Exhibit,* Chrysler Motors Buildings, 1939 New York World's Fair. (*Raymond Loewy/William Snaith, Inc.*)

the last airplane had flown across the screen, a series of spotlights sent beams out to other model planets. Twinkling lights and the hum of motors indicated the one-hour-long New York-to-London space flight was loading. Models of streamlined ships, trains and taxis arrived at the port, and elevators rose to the spacecraft cabins. Warning sirens were heard, and a magnetic crane hoisted the Rocketship and lowered it into the breach of the Rocketgun. After a brief silence there was a flash, a muffled explosion, and the ship vanished into the night! [16] No doubt there were skeptics who totally discounted space travel and others who thought it might be possible in the twenty-fifth century. But suborbital flight as Loewy described it came to pass within three decades after the opening of the Fair. The technology differed, of course, but space travel was far from science fiction.

One company did sponsor a project with the year 6939 A.D. in mind. The Westinghouse Corporation created a time capsule of "cupaloy," a special alloy of copper, chromium and silver, meant to last for five thousand years. In it they placed, in a sealed glass tube, books, photographs and films showing life and the state of progress in 1939. The subjects were contemporary architecture, modern machines and processes, entertainment and communications, and scientific and medical knowledge. Westinghouse proclaimed to future archeologists that

> . . . our engineers and inventors have harnessed the forces of the earth and skies and the mysteries of nature to make our lives pleasant, swift, safe, and fascinating beyond any previous age. We fly faster, higher and farther than the birds. On steel rails we rush safely, behind giant horses of metal and fire. Ships large as palaces thrum across our seas. Our roads are alive with self-propelling conveyances so complex the most powerful prince could not have owned one a generation ago; yet in our day there is hardly a man so poor he cannot afford this form of personal mobility.[17]

The documents were sealed in the 7-foot polished streamlined capsule (fig. 165), and on September 23, 1938, at high noon, the capsule was gently lowered into a 50-foot shaft on the site of the Westinghouse exhibit. As the Streamlined Decade neared its end, its accomplishments were carefully recorded for posterity. The surface of the capsule was inscribed with the request that "if anyone should come upon this capsule before the year A.D. 6939 let him not wantonly disturb it, for to do so would be to deprive the people of that era the legacy here left them." [18]

165. The Westinghouse Corporation Time Capsule, 1939 New York World's Fair. (*Courtesy The Westinghouse Corporation.*)

## THE ARCHITECTURE OF OPTIMISM

The focal exhibits of the 1939 New York World's Fair were designed around a theme promoting an optimistic vision of the future. Their message was that the good will and cooperation of men, combined with the advances of science and technology, could be directed to the building of a cleaner, safer, more efficient and happier tomorrow. That vision was the latest of a series of utopian plans that dated as far back as the ancient Greek philosophers. It was modern in its stress on materialistic solutions to man's problems. Older utopias had been based on the notion that institutions and regulations could control society and make it harmonious. Personal happiness was thought to be dependent upon self-discipline, moral and ethical values and a shared commitment to goals. Since the industrial revolution began in England, late in the eighteenth century, more and more utopian literature has emphasized the role of technology. The machine, in the modern version, will free man from his drudgery, and he will be free to spend his leisure time creatively. Personal contentment has become identified with work-saving devices and features in homes and with the pleasures afforded by improved communications and transportation.

However temporary, the 1939 New York World's Fair showed that intelligent planning and decisive action could result in a clean, spacious, well-landscaped urban design with a reasonably consistent modern style of architecture. It could not be a utopia in the true sense for it had no citizens. Nor could it show the architecture of the future. It did *represent* the architecture of the future with a style generally associated in the public mind with modernity. The World's Fair Moderne was a sculptural style with simple undecorated surfaces. It was clean and light-toned and generally dramatic. The Fair's temporary nature allowed considerable latitude and occasional excesses (the nautical analogy surfaced in the transportation zone) but these were mostly in smaller commercial exhibits. Some buildings were more successful than others, but the lasting impression was of the whole. Sometimes it induced negative reactions:

> *Compare with your nearest Shoe Shoppe. Part of this Fair is the same. There is also a newer kind of over-streamlined pseudo-modern (see the soft corners and fungoid bulges on the buildings by some of our most celebrated industrial designers). This may be called* modernoid.[19]

The editors of *The Architectural Forum* were far less caustic. They found the Fair harmonious in shape and color and felt it had avoided "Chicago's modernistic excesses." [20] (By this they meant the Zigzag Moderne of the 1933 Century of Progress Exposition. At *that* fair, modernism had been a fetish. Exhibit buildings competed with each other for attention and all lost to Sally Rand and her fan dance.) The editors found a number of distinguished buildings at the 1939 Fair but found many more that were, at best, innocuous and felt the desire for overall harmony had led to inoffensive, uniform mediocrity in the official structures.[21] The advanced nature of the exhibition techniques were, they said, perhaps more significant than the architecture, but all in all, they found it a great fair, superlative entertainment by day and enchanting at night.

Perhaps after all, the best analysis is one which considers the whole effect and ignores the lesser defects. As a whole the Fair identified the good life with progress and planning. It did not dwell on current social and economic woes but did express faith in man's abilities to build a better society. It urged that imagination and creativity be applied to problems and promised rewards for cooperative effort. Pleasant homes, safe and fast travel, personal mobility, freedom from drudgery, and the stimulating environment of great cities were among the goals, rewards in themselves. Best of all it provided pleasure (and distraction from the chaos outside the Fair) while educating people in the fundamentals of chemistry, physics, electronics, agriculture, mechanics and home economics.

The new industrial designers had presented both visions and realities, proving their ability in long-range planning and in finding solutions to problems of daily needs. Together with architects, they created a temporary city to amuse, educate and impress the populace. Outside, there was concern about the war developing in Europe which was to delay the realization of the World of Tomorrow. Inside the fairgrounds, however, one could find much to buoy the spirits.

# IX.
# DYNAMIC
# CONTINUUMS

## DYNAMIC FUNCTIONALISM

Functionalist thought has been traced back as far as Socrates, who identified the beautiful with the useful in both architecture and the industrial arts.[1] In the modern period, the industrial revolution presented a new set of problems for the designer, who now had to choose between a style imitative of those developed in the handicrafts or one more nearly reflecting the facts of machine production. The functional designs of the 1920s were largely geometric, an outcome of modern German design under the influence of Cubism, Constructivism and other modern movements. The new machine aesthetic was manifest in simple enameled or polished metal stereometric forms. The absence of surface ornament or literal references was a demonstration of the designer's serious intent to provide a low-cost, durable and sensible product. Often these resembled the machines that had produced them. Geometry had become the ordering system, and the justification for its use was found in the dialogues of Plato:

*By beauty of shapes I do not mean, as most people would suppose, the beauty of living figures or of pictures, but, to make my point clear, I mean straight lines and circles, and shapes, plane or solid, made from them by lathe, ruler and square. These are not, like other things, beautiful relatively, but always and absolutely.[2]*

Americans were introduced to the new machine aesthetic by periodicals and by exhibitions, the most influential of which was held in 1934. Among the items chosen for the Museum of Modern Art's "Machine Art" show were precision laboratory instruments, drafting and surveying equipment, plumbing fixtures, cash registers, safes and kitchen tools. The inclusion of ball bearings, springs, boat propellers and other mundane hardware as "art" also created a stir. Such items of sterile functional beauty were thought by some to be more for the "cerebral aesthete" than for the average person who might reasonably make some emotional demands upon art.[3] Coming as it did in 1934, a banner year in the history of streamlined design, the Machine Art exhibit must have had mixed effects. On the one hand it reinforced the aesthetic appreciation of machines and machine-made objects. On the other hand its geometric forms were in opposition to the organic forms of modernity that appeared that same year: the *Zephyr* and *City of Salinas* streamliners, the *DC–2* aircraft and the *Airflow* and *Dymaxion Car Number Three*. The Museum of Modern Art was a five-year-old upstart in 1934, noted for its avant-garde positions. Curiously, in its Machine Art exhibition the museum had endorsed the forms of an earlier decade, when architecture, and especially the skyscraper, had reigned as the dominant symbol of the modern age.[4] The new transport designs were more closely attuned to the vitality and mobility of life than were the static functional forms developed for architecture. The identification of streamlining with efficiency and sensible design struck a responsive chord among those seeking forms appropriate to the sober days of the Depression. The vitality of the new forms promised a change from stagnant modes of thought and provided an emotional outlet lacking in geometric forms.

## THE AESTHETICS OF SHELLS

The streamlined products created by the leading American designers of the 1930s were largely free of surface ornament. The designers generally eschewed motifs, with the exception of parallel bands. Art Deco designers had relied upon graphic motifs like skyscrapers, Zeppelins and automobiles to convey the notion of modernity, and these were used in a decorative manner. This pastiche of imagery and pseudo-cubist forms was a far cry from the sincere geometric designs of the Bauhaus. Streamlined designs

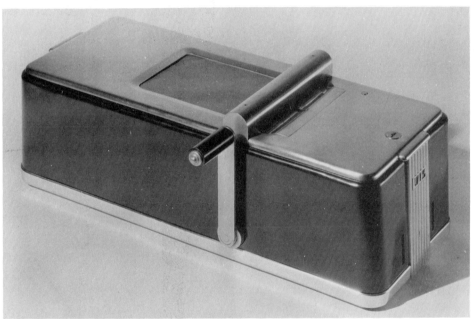

166. The American Sales Book Wiz Register before (ABOVE) and after (BELOW) re-designing by Walter Dorwin Teague in 1934. (*Walter Dorwin Teague Associates, Inc.*)

symbolized the age by incorporating transportation *principles* into their forms rather than by presenting vehicles graphically.

In the 1930s many products were redesigned that had retained their earliest forms. Some rather dramatic redesigns were possible when the original design, however functional, had an "antique" look about it. One case in point was the *Wiz* register remodeled for the American Sales Book Company in 1934 by Walter Dorwin Teague (fig. 166). Screws, a pebbled texture and slots detracted from the appearance of the original. The exposed mechanism seemed to invite the ruffled sleeve of a saleslady's blouse. Teague updated the mechanism and cleanlined its shell, giving it a unified and neatly detailed appearance. Raymond Loewy accomplished the same thing in his 1939 redesign of the International Harvester cream separator (fig. 167), a product that demands maximum cleanliness and ease of maintenance. The simplified polished shells that enveloped these designs conveyed literally the idea of sanitation; the attention being given hygiene was a major consideration for designers of the decade.

New plastic materials were particularly suited to streamlined designs. Organic forms with rounded edges were less likely to develop in-

167. Raymond Loewy. International Harvest Cream Separator. Before (LEFT) and after (RIGHT) redesign in 1939. (*Raymond Loewy/William Snaith, Inc.*)

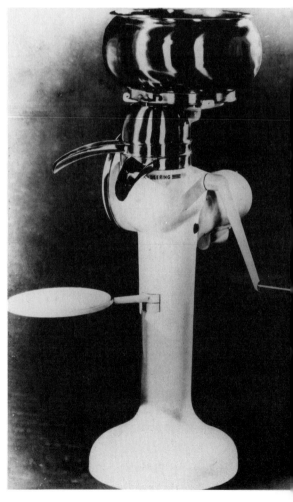

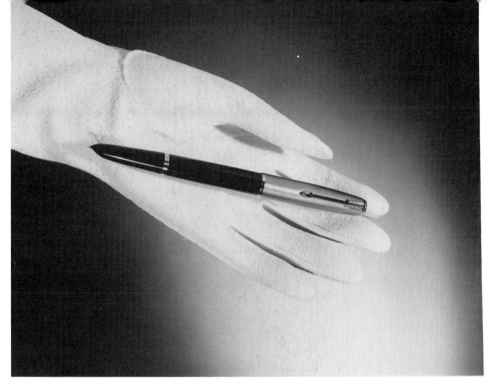

168. Marlin Baker, Joseph Platt and Kenneth Parker. The Parker *51* Pen. 1939. (*Courtesy the Parker Pen Company.*)

ternal stresses that could lead to cracking of the shell.[5] The noted educator Laszlo Moholy-Nagy recognized that even stationary objects might be streamlined to facilitate mass production processes like stamping, casting and molding because the rounded edges eased production and finishing.[6] He particularly admired the *Parker 51* pen introduced in 1939 (fig. 168) for the company's fifty-first anniversary. The pen was not styled, but designed from scratch to use a new quick-drying ink the company had developed. The Lucite barrel was designed for the human hand and naturally assumed an organic form.

## SYMBOL VS. FUNCTION

Much of the criticism leveled against streamlining centered on the presumed misapplication of aerodynamic principles to stationary objects. The *cause célèbre* among design critics seems to have been a pencil sharpener encased in a chrome-plated teardrop shell. Dreyfuss and others deplored it as an "absurdity." [7] Admittedly the teardrop became a design cliché, but in discussing streamlined objects Siegfried Giedion pointed out that "it is only natural that an age of movement should adopt a form associated with movement as its symbol, using it in all places at all occasions." [8] Talented designers recognized the need for an authentic style as a unifying device, one that explains and gives coherence to an age. For the 1920s, the skyscraper provided an authentic symbol and inspired an angular style that expressed the tempo of the Jazz Age. Such spurious Art Deco motifs as fountains and sunrays were fashionable but transitory. The teardrop and related forms were a sincere expression of a shift in the 1930s to a more sober mood and a desire for more efficiency and productivity.[9]

## DYNAMIC CONTINUUMS

This essay began with the contention that streamlined forms reflect a general interest in smooth, efficient and continuous motion in the twentieth century. An aesthetic of continuums can refer to designed objects—like the freeway which provides such motion—or to the design goals themselves. One function of urban planning, for example, is to provide the efficient flow of goods, traffic, energy and information. Disruptions in those systems make urban life chaotic and unpleasant.

Examples can be drawn from other disciplines as well. In literature, the "stream-of-consciousness" technique has been used to reveal the psychic being of a fictitious character. It first appeared as an "interior monologue" in Edouard Dujardin's *Les lauriers sont coupés* (1887). In this century the technique has been used to project an endless flow of sensations, thoughts, memories and associations on all levels of awareness.[10] The arrangement of thoughts is not necessarily logical for the pattern is determined by the process of associations, but the flow itself is continuous and fluid. James Joyce, Virginia Woolf and William Faulkner were notable practitioners of the technique in the 1920s and 1930s.[11] Molly Bloom's unspoken soliloquy in Joyce's *Ulysses,* notorious in its day for its sexual content, provided a dynamic, uninterrupted effect equivalent to streamlining in design. In it Molly reviews her day's experiences and anticipates the future, both of which trigger associations from the past. Her thoughts glide from one to the next as her consciousness sinks to lower levels of awareness, being absorbed finally in sleep.

William James provided the term "stream of consciousness" in his *Principles of Psychology* (1890). James found the words "chain" or "train" inappropriate descriptions of consciousness, preferring the metaphors "river" or "stream." [12] The flow does not proceed at a uniform pace but seems to be an alternation of flights and perchings, like a bird's life.[13] The rhythm of our language expresses this, each thought being expressed in a sentence. Periods which close each sentence mark the beginning not of a disruption or cessation of thought, but of a sort of resting place occupied by sensorial imaginations. These "substantive parts" between the transitive sentences afford a moment of contemplation.[14]

Our sense organs, wrote James, are confronted with the physical environment which appears to be a "swarming *continuum*" of movements, events and things lacking distinction and emphasis. Depending on our practical or aesthetic interests, our senses make selections from this flow, giving certain things prominence and ignoring the rest.[15] Experience is subjective and depends upon one's habits of attention, i.e., his preferences or needs determine which things or events are selected.[16] In the stream-of-consciousness novel the range and selection of thoughts reveal the psychic character of the thinker which may not be explained by his actions and verbalizations. In dealing with the process of association, James drew an example from Jane Austen's *Emma* (1816) in which a character "redintegrates" or reconstructs a situation through recall.[17] James found that association proceeded from thing to thing rather than idea to idea.[18]

Henri Bergson recognized a duality in the nature of consciousness. One aspect is its unity and continuity; no feelings, ideas or volitions exist without constantly evolving. While they are being experienced, they have no apparent beginnings or endings; they appear as a flux of evolving shades, as though one were passing through a spectrum.[19] They occur in *duration*, a temporal continuum which is known intuitively. Our selective attention distinguishes and separates them artificially into discrete particles, the "multiplicity" that contradicts the sense of continuity.[20] But this second, opposing aspect of consciousness is limited and relative for it arises from conception. Intuition, by contrast, can reveal the dynamic, qualitative, concrete reality.

John Dewey took a position reflecting James's analysis of the thought process and reiterating Bergson's metaphysics of process. He regarded *experience* as a smooth continuum. Of particularly traumatic or memorable experience he wrote that

> . . . *every successive part flows freely, without seam and without unfilled blanks, into what ensues. At the same time there is no sacrifice of the self-identity of the parts. . . . Because of continuous merging, there are no holes, mechanical junctions, and dead centers when we have an* experience. *There are no pauses, places of rest, but they punctuate and define the quality of movement. They sum up what has been undergone and prevent its dissipation and idle evaporation. Continued acceleration is breathless and prevents parts from gaining distinction. In a work of art, different acts, episodes, occurrences melt and fuse into a unity, and yet do not disappear and lose their character as they do so. . . .*[21]

Dewey expressed these thoughts in lectures at Harvard in 1931; they were published three years later, the year of the *Zephyr* and the *Airflow*. Their emphasis on movement, continuous flow and the absorption of parts into the whole is analogous to streamlining in design, where they might describe a smooth teardrop shell.

Modern filmmaking techniques can provide a continuum of experience. By "dissolving" one scene into another, filming from a moving boom or dolly, or zooming into or out from a scene, cinematographers can avoid abrupt changes of scene or camera angle. The result is a greater continuity in the narrative and often a sense of immediacy. Special high-speed cameras have been used to slow down what would otherwise be chaotic, staccato action to the pace of a graceful ballet, providing a deeper comprehension of an event.

The American industrial engineer Frank Gilbreth used still and motion pictures to analyze the movements of workers to better understand their work patterns. Gilbreth was an advocate of scientific management and an enemy of methods that wasted energy. By 1917 he had developed the Cyclegraph method of motion study in which a small electric light was attached to the hand or other part of the worker. The motion was then recorded on photographic film in stereoscopic cameras, providing a three-dimensional record.[22] By interrupting the current through the bulb at regular intervals he was able to create a "line of time spots" which clocked each component of the motion.[23] Lillian Gilbreth described a 1914 Stereocyclograph of a surgeon tying a knot as "the beautiful smooth repetitive pattern of the expert."[24] Gilbreth formed wire "motion models" based on the photographs and used these as aids in training workers.[25] His concern for efficiency and his studies that led to the smoothing out and simplification of motion paths suggest a close parallel with those who developed modern aerodynamics. The continuums he orchestrated for workers were practical and humane; they increased productivity while reducing fatigue.

Kinetic sculpture has provided continuums of visual experience. Alexander Calder's suspended *mobiles*, propelled by air currents, drift through cyclic paths sometimes in a varying pattern but always in smooth, continuous movements. José De Rivera's *Construction No. 72* (fig. 169) is a graceful curve of stainless steel tubing that revolves slowly on a motorized base. In motion it vitalizes and articulates its ambient space. The clarity of its surface mirrors the environment and provides a path for reflected lights, which appear to glide endlessly along the moving structure. As the piece turns through its cycle, it presents a constantly changing profile; the large radius appears to fold back upon itself and the tapered ends follow, drawn through an imaginary loop. The array glides silently past the viewer and the cycle begins again. De Rivera has fashioned smaller continuous loops without motors or pivots, but even these suggest movement. It

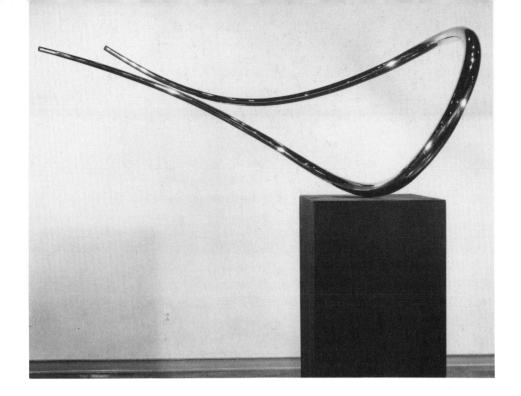

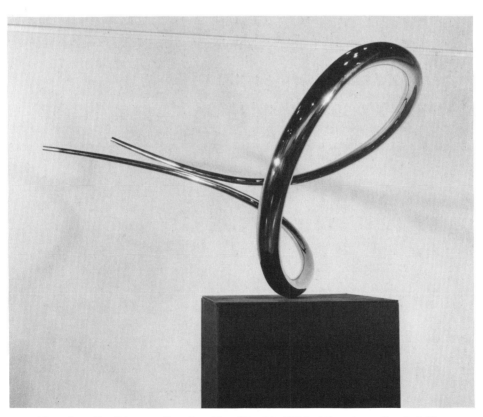

169a&b.  Jose De Rivera. *Construction No. 72.* 1960. (*Courtesy the Art Museum, University of New Mexico, Albuquerque.*)

is as though he had added the dimension of time to Gilbreth's wire schema, transforming them from static records to graceful performers.

In his collected essays on "What is American about America," John A. Kouwenhoven lists several items indigenous to our culture. Included are the grid plan for cities, the skyscraper, Jazz, comic strips, soap operas, assembly-line production and chewing gum.[26] All are examples of extendable and repeatable systems-in-progress. They are typically American in their dynamism and in being subject to change. As such they are useful in illustrating the dynamic flux of the nation as a whole and in explaining the interest in streamlining among Americans struggling against the viscosity of a Depression that had checked their forward progress.

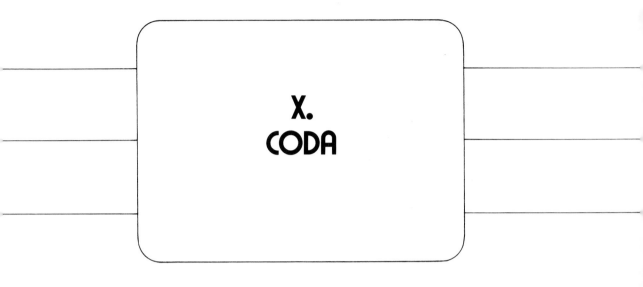

# X.
# CODA

## THE CLASSICAL PERIOD OF MODERN DESIGN

In retrospect, the streamlined era of the 1930s can be seen as the classical period of twentieth-century design. It was immediately preceded by an archaic period and was followed by mannerist and baroque periods. The archaic period of the 1920s produced rigid, formal designs and a geometric, static machine aesthetic identified with de Stijl, Constructivism and the Bauhaus. Designers of the archaic period avoided not only ornament but organic forms in general. Their approach was conceptual and their synthetic forms, rationalized through mathematics, offered only cerebral pleasure. The sterility of these designs stemmed from the dominance of thinking and the exclusion of feeling. In their adulation of machine forms, archaic designers overlooked the spirit of the machine and failed to express the dynamism of the age.

American designers of the classical period, like their nineteenth-century predecessors, were open to the suggestions of science and practical technologies but were unrestricted by aesthetic canons or tradition. In the spirit of economy that has always marked American vernacular forms, they promoted and adapted aerodynamics to vehicular designs thereby imparting to them the vitality of organic forms. By containing machines in simple envelopes they created a new aesthetic and an appropriate new symbol of dynamism. Thinking and feeling were reunited in forms that revealed their function while expressing the emotional thrust of the decade—the desire for swift, smooth travel. Designers of the classical period must be credited with tempering rational engineering with the artist's instinct for beautiful form.

The evolution of design was interrupted during the first half of the next decade as the war created a demand for products in which performance was the only requirement and aesthetics played no part. In the latter half of the 1940s, consumer products reappeared that vaguely resembled designs of the classical period. In this postwar mannerist period automobile designers echoed the forms of the streamlined period but only as a superficial application, for styling had replaced design. As automobiles became more plentiful, the stylist played an increasingly important role in the competition for sales. By the mid-1950s, auto styling produced voluptuous baroque forms quite unlike the simple teardrop shells envisioned in the 1930s. Auto forms exhibited a tremendous degree of plasticity with fishtails, swept wings and bulging curves. Surfaces were encrusted with chromium ornaments that resembled and recalled rockets, wings, boosters and other aircraft parts. Streamlining was now interpreted as a purely visual effect meant to recall *supersonic* flight. Aside from the debated claims of stability offered by tail fins, there were no radical improvements in design. After several more years, autos had become increasingly larger, more powerful, more garish and more expensive to operate. The public began to react by buying the simple, rear-engined, partly streamlined Volkswagen, little changed from the classical period. American manufacturers responded with the "compact" car, and the cycle was complete. Some buyers and most manufacturers had aligned their thinking with the classical designers of the 1930s, and smaller, more economical and hence more democratic automobiles were produced in the 1960s.

## THE CLASSICAL DESIGNS

Several designs of the Streamlined Decade are indisputably "classic" in the sense that they continue to command respect. Among them is Geddes's *Ocean Liner,* a bold and total application of fluid dynamics that acknowledged the importance of both wind and wave resistance. It is regrettable that this handsome teardrop form, modified only by its bridge and stacks, was not advanced beyond the planning stage. Geddes would

have provided luxury, convenience and perhaps greater safety while short-
ening the transatlantic voyage. The Douglas *DC–3* proved one of the most
stable and useful of aircraft in transporting personnel and cargo. Its
basic form affected fuselage design through the era of piston engines and
into the jet age. The application of aerodynamics provided both economy
and a symbolic form that significantly affected other vehicular designs.

The Burlington *Zephyr* was a reconsideration of railroad motive
power, one brought about by the diesel engine resulting in increased economy and efficiency. Uninhibited by the traditions of steam locomotive design, the *Zephyr*'s designers rearranged the cab for greater visibility and
provided a low center of gravity, light weight and aerodynamic streamlining. Like the *DC–3*, the polished stainless steel exterior was easy to maintain and provided a machine aesthetic suited to the decade. Loewy's *GG–1*
broke from the tradition of boxy electric engines cluttered with rivets,
joints and windows. He clustered the cabs at the center of the symmetrical units and employed welding to cut assembly costs, while providing the
smooth envelope that had become the hallmark of streamlined design. One
of the finest of the streamlined steam engines was Dreyfuss's *Twentieth-
Century Limited*. Like Loewy's *GG–1*, its simple exterior made visual coherence out of a complex machine, and thereby increased its clarity as a
symbol of modern progressive rail travel. Dreyfuss restricted his vocabulary of forms and avoided the mannerisms that became clichés in the
hands of lesser designers. The engine was trim but aggressive in appearance. Its success was due in part to the fact that it was not a redesign but
one Dreyfuss could coordinate from the very beginning.

Fuller's *Dymaxion Cars* were unique in their application of aerodynamic principles and aircraft fabrication techniques. They were the
first true teardrop automobiles seen by Americans. They represented the
first total reconsideration of road vehicles since the four-wheel type had
been established. In the *Dymaxion Cars*, the engineer's parsimony and
good sense resulted in a form that industrial designers had also found
aesthetically pleasing. The 1937 *Volkswagen* combined some of Jaray's aerodynamic principles with an economical chassis to provide low-cost transportation. The car, little changed in appearance, continues to attract those
wanting cheap transportation free of stylistic devices that encourage obsolescence. Like the *Dymaxion Cars*, it is a statement on the nature of the
automobile made by the engineer, not the stylist. The Lincoln *Continental*, though not a teardrop form, featured many of the basic techniques of
streamlining. The running boards and rear wheels were contained within
the body shell, the headlights were recessed within the front fenders which
blended smoothly with the hood, and the rear fenders were partially ab-

sorbed into the body. The restrained use of ornament, the large expanses of contoured, polished surface, and the trim proportions gave the car a lithe and graceful appearance in keeping with the spirit of streamlined design.

## THE RISE AND FALL OF THE TEARDROP

One can cite figures to demonstrate the futility of streamlining at low speeds or the superiority of Dr. Kamm's truncated teardrop, but this information was not available to the designers for most of the decade. Within the framework of available data, they based their work on presumptions later subject to question. This is the natural process in the sciences, and any significant scientist of the past can be unfairly criticized for acting within his limitations. Some designers, however, did fail to grasp the inevitability of change when they projected the teardrop as an ultimate form. Geddes and Teague spoke of the teardrop as a kind of platonic ideal to be achieved, a final solution to transportation design. The notion was as restrictive as those of de Stijl designers and tended to control the style of the 1930s. The presumption was that aerodynamic efficiency alone would determine the basic forms of transportation, particularly the automobile. In a democratic society, however, the consumer does not always respond to logical arguments.

In addition to the desire for novelty and change in America, the other factors that render "ultimate" designs obsolete are 1) innovations in materials, fabrication methods and tools which help to shape forms and create new potentials for designers, 2) the emergence of new functional and performance requirements, and 3) changing social conditions and attitudes which the designer expresses through new forms. In light of the economic and political upheavals of the 1930s, the notion of an ultimate form appears in retrospect to have been a naive one.

## STREAMLINED FORMS AS SYMBOLS

Man-made streamlined objects first took the form of projectiles, ships' hulls, submarines, Zeppelins, hydroplanes, racing cars and aircraft. Many appeared before the 1930s, and all were associated with high speed, efficiency and daring exploits. They were clear, memorable forms that inevitably came to denote progress and modernity. The logic of streamlining was so self-evident that its transference from aircraft to other vehicles was a natural step, but one accomplished more easily in public transportation—trains, streetcars and buses—than in the private automobile. Acceptance of the streamlined automobile came later and more slowly, apparently because of the reluctance of the public to make a major investment and an open commitment to a radical idea.

Streamlining is a useful metaphor for the interests and life-style of Americans following 1929. Shaken by the market failure, the country took a more responsible and sober course than it had in the previous decade. The open car associated with the reckless pace of the Roaring Twenties gave way to the closed car of the thirties, a vehicle better suited to efficiency than to wild abandon. Frivolity in the decorative arts was discarded for symbols of sensible economy: the smooth, undecorated Streamlined Moderne. Hot jazz music was superseded by the relaxed undulations of "Swing" tempo. The high-rising verticality of the skyscraper, with the nervous vitality of its profile, fell to the sleek, low, horizontal transportation design as the dominant symbol of the modern age. As engineers and designers sought new solutions for industry's malaise, New Deal politicians wrote experimental legislation to accelerate the economy. The laissez-faire philosophy had discredited itself and the watchword was decisive action. The new administration sought to instill confidence in the future and in the forward progress of the nation. The streamlined teardrop was emblematic of that goal.

## NOTES ON STYLE

The widespread application of streamlining and the uniformity of appearance among a variety of products, from trains to radios, resulted from two factors. First, there was the shared interest in the technical and symbolic value of streamlining, that is, in its rational and evocative qualities. As a metaphor for progress, streamlining had gained such currency that by 1935 a "streamlined" product could convey the modernity associated with the *Zephyr* or the *DC–3*. Secondly, there was an adaptation of materials and processes from one industry to another that contributed to the convergence of forms. The *Zephyr's* lightweight alloy construction is closer to aircraft technology than traditionally heavy iron locomotive fabrication. Fuller initiated such transference in his *Dymaxion Cars* and later had his 1944 *Dymaxion Dwelling Machine* fabricated at an aircraft plant. The increasing use of plastics in small products also led to "streamlined" forms because rounded corners relieve stresses in injection-molded forms. These molded forms served as ashtrays, automobile knobs, radio dials and utensil handles. Their similarity, a result of a technological process, lent uniformity to a variety of design problems.

Beginning in the early 1930s, industrial designers began providing Americans with a greater awareness of sculptural form. Streamlining cleansed the surfaces of their two-dimensional ornamental patterns and directed attention to the plastic qualities of three-dimensional form. As useful objects, streamlined designs were necessarily abstract forms. Their organic quality evoked an association with natural forms and with modern biomorphic sculpture. This provided the emotional experience lacking in geometric machine art of the previous decade.

The consideration of industrial design as a vehicle of artistic expression and a source of aesthetic experience is neither improper nor illogical. The industrial designer and the architect are in a better position than the painter or sculptor to provide visual and tactile experiences that enrich daily life. Design and architecture are not confined to galleries and museums; the public come in daily contact with all manner of useful objects, from tableware to sports equipment, and they experience architecture as dwellers, shoppers, worshipers and workers. The major part of their aesthetic experience is derived from their daily environment and is accumulated almost subliminally, that is, without the dispositions assumed by the museum visitor. While the museum rarely offers more than visual experience, the coordinated environment of the automobile, the home, church or shopping mall provide tactile, auditory, and occasionally olfactory enjoyment as well.

Because of their responsibility in shaping the environment, the designer and the architect must find the means to harmonize its elements. This will be accomplished as they become capable of identifying the concerns, attitudes and motivations of society and expressing these with suitable motifs and forms derived from appropriate design principles. The leading designers of the 1930s were prevented from creating total visual order, given the limited scope of their activities and the prevailing economic situation. They did, however, consistently apply streamlining principles to the individual components. As a result, many of the classic designs of the streamlined era have a harmonious similarity—an authentic style derived from the conditions of the times. The artifacts of any period worthy of study tend to have a consistent style. For the United States of the 1930s, streamlining provided the distinctive identifying style, and an understanding of this design principle provides an important dimension to the history of the period.

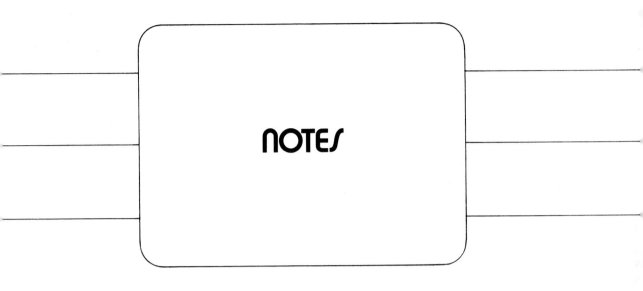

## I. INTRODUCTION

1. Superhighways are not low-resistance forms developed in wind-tunnel testing but they evolved from the need to provide a continuous function. Efficiency and speed are the goals common to the design of "streamlined" systems and streamlined vehicles.

2. Notably those for whom functionalism implied geometric forms and a prohibition against ornament. The movement had its greatest proponents among de Stijl architects in Holland and at the Bauhaus, a German school of architecture and design. By the mid-1930s the style they had created—boxy glass and steel buildings—was being called the International Style, and the rigid vocabulary of sparse cubic forms had acquired the status of a canon. See Nikolaus Pevsner, *Pioneers of Modern Design from William Morris to Walter Gropius,* rev. ed. (Harmondsworth, Middlesex, England: Penguin Books, 1960) and Reyner Banham, *Theory and Design in the First Machine Age,* 2nd ed. (New York: Praeger, 1967).

3. The "teardrop," rounded at the front and tapered at the rear, approximates the low-resistance forms of Zeppelins, submarines and other streamlined vehicles. Rolling down a cheek, a tear *does* assume that form; a falling drop

187

of water does not. The two were confused throughout the decade. The author will use the term, as designers did, in reference to the form described above. Airfoils are similar but their shapes provide lift as well as low resistance.

4. The distinction between *designing* and *styling* must be made. Designing involves an examination of all parameters of a design problem and the development of a form to satisfy the needed functions. Unique requirements lead, in this situation, to unique forms. Styling, on the other hand, is often a superficial alteration of the exterior, meant to give a product market appeal. The stylist imposes a preconceived form upon an existing product, while the designer allows function to dictate form. In fact few of the pioneer industrial designers were exclusively designers or stylists.

Style itself is defined here as the distinctive characteristic or set of characteristics of forms from a given period. It can result naturally from similar solutions to similar problems or it can be imposed deliberately. The characteristics of streamlined forms evolved from known scientific principles which, by the end of the 1930s, had become exploited and were misapplied to extend the style.

## II. THE SCIENCE OF PENETRATION

1. R. GIACOMELLI and E. PISTOLESI, "Historical Sketch," *Aerodynamic Theory: A General Review of Progress,* ed. William F. Durand (New York: Dover, 1963), vol. I, p. 315.

2. A. M. ROBB, "The Development of Applied Hydrodynamics," *A History of Technology: The Late Nineteenth Century,* ed. C. Singer et al. (Oxford: The Clarendon Press, 1958), vol. V, p. 387.

3. ASCHER, H. SHAPIRO, *Shape and Flow: The Fluid Dynamics of Drag* (Garden City, N.Y.: Anchor Books, 1961), p. 148. The motion is relative; either the body or the fluid may move. Even a streamlined body is subject to additional drag force along the surface, although a highly polished surface is less subject to drag than a rough one.

4. GIACOMELLI and PISTOLESI, p. 334. Rankine's work of 1864 involved the study of ships' water lines. For these curves he proposed the term "Neoids" derived from the Greek word for shipshape curves.

5. SIR GEORGE CAYLEY, "Essay upon the Mechanical Principles of Aerial Navigation" (1804), quoted in Charles H. Gibbs-Smith, *Sir George Cayley's Aeronautics, 1796–1855* (London: H.M.S.O., 1962), p. 13. Cayley was the first theorist to divorce the system of lift from the system of thrust, a concept leading to the development of powered fixed-wing aircraft.

6. *Ibid.,* p. 41.

7. *Ibid.,* p. 57. In 1850 Cayley devised a whirling-arm apparatus for testing streamlined forms in motion and for evaluating airfoil sections. See Gibbs-Smith, pp. 143–146.

8. N. H. RANDERS-PEHRSON, "Pioneer Wind Tunnels," *Smithsonian Misc. Coll.,* vol. XCIII, no. 4 (Jan. 1935), pp. 5, 6. The study of lift was a coequal goal of wind-tunnel researchers.

9. *Ibid.*

10. SIEGFRIED GIEDION, *Mechanization Takes Command* (New York: W. W. Norton, 1969), pp. 18–24.

11. RANDERS-PEHRSON, pp. 8, 9.

12. Prime sources for the history of the study of animal locomotion are Marey's *La Methode Graphique dans les sciences expérimentales* (1885), *Du mouvement dans les fonctions de la vie* (1868), *Le vol des oiseaus* (1890) and his last book, *Le mouvement* (1894); Muybridge's *Animal Locomotion,* 11 vols. (1887); and Gilbreth's *Motion Study* (1911), *Fatigue Study* (with Lillian Gilbreth) and *Applied Motion Study* (1917).

13. C. E. ROSENDAHL, *What about the Airship?* (New York: Chas. Scribner's Sons, 1938), p. 47.

14. See ALBERTO SANTOS-DUMONT, *My Airships* (New York: Dover, 1973) and John Toland, *The Great Dirigibles* (New York: Dover, 1972), which was originally published by Henry Holt and Co. in 1957 as *Ships in the Sky.*

15. RANDERS-PEHRSON, p. 7.

16. PETER W. BROOKS, "Aeronautics," *A History of Technology: The Late Nineteenth Century,* vol. V, p. 402.

17. For further reading in the history of aerodynamics, see Theodore von Kármán, *Aerodynamics: Selected Topics in the Light of Their Historical Development* (Ithaca: Cornell Univ. Press, 1954).

18. SIR D'ARCY WENTWORTH THOMPSON, *On Growth and Form,* 2 vols., 2nd ed. reprinted (Cambridge, England: The Syndics of the Cambridge Univ. Press, 1963), vol. II, p. 941. The first edition was published in 1917.

19. *Ibid.,* p. 961.

20. *Ibid.,* p. 965.

21. *Ibid.,* vol. I, p. 16.

22. *Ibid.,* vol. II, p. 966.

23. HERBERT READ, *A Concise History of Modern Sculpture* (New York: Praeger, 1964), p. 80.

24. CAROLA GIEDION-WELCKER, *Constantin Brancusi,* trans. by Maria Jolas and Anne Leroy (New York: George Braziller, 1959), p. 23.

25. ATHENA T. SPEAR, *Brancusi's Birds* (New York: New York Univ. Press, 1969), p. 25. Technologists measure surface refinement and have a mathematical scale with which to prescribe flatness and the degree of coarseness or smoothness. Brancusi probably failed to specify his needs.

26. *Ibid.*, p. 36.

27. Brancusi quoted in Malvina Hoffman, *Sculpture Inside and Out,* reprint of 1939 ed. (New York: Bonanza Books, n.d.), p. 54.


### III. IDEAL FORMS

1. W. FRANCKLYN PARIS, *French Arts and Letters and Other Essays* (Port Washington, N.Y.: Kennikat Press, 1968), p. 110.

2. See BEVIS HILLIER, *Art Deco* (Minneapolis: Minn. Institute of the Arts, 1971), p. 39.

3. "Color in Industry," *Fortune,* vol. I, no. 1 (Feb. 1930), p. 85.

4. LEWIS MUMFORD, *Modern Architects* (New York: Museum of Modern Art, 1932), p. 183.

5. CHARLES MERZ, *And Then Came Ford* (Garden City, N.Y.: Doubleday, Doran and Co., 1929), pp. 282, 283.

6. SEYMOUR FREEDGOOD, "Odd Business, This Industrial Design," *Fortune,* vol. LIX, no. 2 (Feb. 1959), p. 132.

7. NORMAN BEL GEDDES, *Horizons* (New York: Random House, 1932), p. 5. Geddes studied briefly at the Cleveland School of Art and the Chicago Institute as a teenager, but he had no other formal art training. His professional experiences prior to becoming an industrial designer are described in his autobiography, *Miracle in the Evening,* ed. Wm. Kelley (New York: Doubleday and Co., Inc., 1960).

8. "Both Fish and Fowl," *Fortune,* vol. IX, no. 2 (Feb. 1934), p. 90.

9. *Ibid.*, p. 94.

10. GEDDES, *Horizons*, p. 251.

11. HENRY DREYFUSS, *Designing For People* (New York: Simon and Schuster, 1955), p. 77.

12. WALTER DORWIN TEAGUE, *Design This Day: The Technique of Order in the Machine Age* (New York: Harcourt, Brace and Co., 1940).

13. RAYMOND LOEWY, *Never Leave Well Enough Alone* (New York: Simon and Schuster, 1951).

14. ROBERT W. MARKS, *The Dymaxion World of Buckminster Fuller* (Carbondale, Ill.: Southern Illinois Univ. Press, 1960), p. 9.

15. RICHARD BUCKMINSTER FULLER, *Ideas and Integrities,* ed. Robert W. Marks (New York: Collier Books, 1969), pp. 9, 10.

16. RICHARD BUCKMINSTER FULLER, *4D Time Lock,* reprint of 1928 ed. (Corrales, N.M.: Lama Foundation, 1970).

17. RICHARD BUCKMINSTER FULLER, *Nine Chains to the Moon* (Carbondale, Ill.: Southern Illinois Univ. Press, 1963).

18. OTTO KUHLER, *My Iron Journey: An Autobiography of a Life with Steam and Steel* (Denver: Intermountain Chapter, National Railway Hist. Soc., 1967).

19. FREDERICK LEWIS ALLEN, *Since Yesterday* (New York: Harper and Row, 1972), pp. 71, 72.

20. ROY SHELDON and EGMONT ARENS, *Consumer Engineering: A New Technique for Prosperity* (New York: Harper and Bros., 1932), p. 169.

21. *Ibid.*

22. *Ibid.*, pp. 43, 44.

23. *Ibid.*, p. 97.

24. *Ibid.*, p. 19.

25. GEDDES, *Horizons*, p. 4.

26. *Ibid.*, pp. 4, 5.

27. *Ibid.*, p. 50.

28. *Ibid.*, p. 227.

29. "Both Fish and Fowl," p. 94.

30. Allen, *Since Yesterday*, p. 7.

31. H. F. KING, *Milestones of the Air: Janes 100 Significant Aircraft*, ed. J. W. R. Taylor (New York: McGraw-Hill, 1969), p. 66.

32. "Both Fish and Fowl," p. 94.

33. GEDDES, *Horizons*, p. 109.

34. R. E. G. DAVIES, "Pan Am's Planes," Part 1, *Air Pictorial*, vol. 29, no. 9 (Sept. 1967), p. 2.

35. *Ibid.*, p. 5.

36. KING, *Milestones of the Air*, p. 80.

37. DAVIES, "Pan Am's Planes," Part 1, p. 6.

38. DAVIES, "Pan Am's Planes," Part 2, *Air Pictorial*, vol. 29, no. 10 (Oct. 1967), p. 8.

39. From a Pan Am press release, n.d.

40. DAVIES, "Pan Am's Planes," Part 2, p. 10.

41. For an evolution of aircraft forms, see *Pedigree of Champions: Boeing Since 1916* (Seattle: The Boeing Co., 1963).

42. ALEXANDER KLEMIN, "The Secret of Aviation Speed," *Scientific American*, vol. CXLIII, no. 5 (Nov. 1930), p. 393.

43. "Douglas DC–1," undated press release, Douglas Aircraft, Santa Monica, California, pp. 1, 2.

44. "Douglas DC–3: Background Information," press release, McDonnell Douglas Corporation, Santa Monica, California, dated 16 May 1972, pp. 2, 3.

45. *Ibid.*

46. LE CORBUSIER (CHARLES EDOUARD JEANNERET), *Towards a New Architecture,* trans. Frederick Etchells, from the 1923 ed. (New York: Praeger, 1960), p. 100.

47. LE CORBUSIER (CHARLES EDOUARD JEANNERET), *Aircraft* (New York: The Studio Publications, 1935), p. 10.

48. SELDON CHENEY and MARTHA CHENEY, *Art and the Machine* (New York: Whittlesey House, 1936), p. 16.

49. GEDDES, *Horizons,* p. 20.

50. TEAGUE, *Design This Day,* p. 165.

51. GEDDES, *Horizons,* pp. 55, 63.

52. TEAGUE, *Design This Day,* p. 106.

53. MARKS, *The Dymaxion World,* p. 27.

## IV. THE DYNAMICS OF TWO FLUIDS: THE STREAMLINED SHIP

1. HORATIO GREENOUGH, "American Architecture" (1843), in *Form and Function: Remarks on Art, Design and Architecture,* ed. Harold Small (Berkeley: Univ. of Calif. Press, 1966), pp. 60, 61.

2. Quoted in JOHN A. KOUWENHOVEN, *The Arts in Modern American Civilization* (New York: W. W. Norton, 1967), p. 29.

3. RALPH WALDO EMERSON, "Thoughts on Art" (1841), *American Art, 1700–1960: Sources and Documents,* John W. McCaulrey, ed., Sources and Documents in the History of Art Series, H. W. Janson, series ed. (Englewood Cliffs, N.J.: Prentice-Hall, 1965), p. 73.

4. *Ibid.,* p. 72.

5. *Ibid.*

6. *Ibid.,* pp. 77, 78.

7. Quoted in HERWIN SCHAEFER, *Nineteenth Century Modern: The Functional Tradition in Victorian Design* (New York: Praeger, 1970), p. 48. In 1865, the English naval architect John Scott Russell wrote about the "line of least resistance." (See Shaefer, p. 47.)

8. LE CORBUSIER, *Towards a New Architecture,* pp. 84–89.

9. The 1925 Paris exposition of decorative arts was to have taken place several years earlier but was delayed by the World War. Le Corbusier's comments were made in 1923 when the exposition was in the planning stage.

10. *Ibid.,* p. 84.

11. *Ibid.,* p. 94.

12. *Ibid.,* pp. 96, 97.

13. JOHN MALCOLM BRINNIN, *The Sway of the Grand Saloon* (New York: Delacorte Press, 1971), p. 386.

14. On one passage, H. E. Huntington, the railway heir, booked the Gainsborough suite and became so enamored of its copy of *The Blue Boy* that he bought the original. See Brinnin, pp. 448, 449.

15. JOHN MAXTONE-GRAHAM, *The Only Way to Cross* (New York: The Macmillan Co., 1972), pp. 112, 117.

16. GEDDES, *Horizons,* pp. 34, 35.

17. A reference, possibly, to the *Ile de France,* the *Bremen,* and the *Europa.*

18. NORMAN BEL GEDDES, "Streamlining," *The Atlantic Monthly,* vol. CLIV, no. 5 (Nov. 1934), pp. 553–563.

19. *Ibid.,* p. 562.

20. *Ibid.,* p. 563. Monocoque construction utilizes the "skin" to carry a large portion of the stresses.

21. NORMAN BEL GEDDES, *Miracle in the Evening,* William Kelley, ed. (New York: Doubleday, 1960), p. 344.

22. GEDDES, *Horizons,* pp. 38, 39.

23. Beginning in 1928, the *Ile de France* began launching a plane about 400 miles from shore in order to save a full day in the delivery of air mail. See Brinnin, *The Sway of the Grand Saloon,* p. 466.

24. *Ibid.,* p. 432.

25. GEDDES, *Horizons,* p. 43. Statistical figures for the *Queen Mary* and the *Queens Elizabeth I* and *II* are found in Leonard A. Stevens, *The Elizabeth: Passage of a Queen* (New York: Knopf, 1968), Appendix A.

26. The *Europa* and her sister ship, the *Bremen,* made the crossing in four days, seventeen hours, forty-two minutes.

27. See MAXTONE-GRAHAM, *The Only Way,* p. 250. The invention is credited to an American, Admiral Taylor, and is in common use today.

28. The short stacks deposited soot on the deck and were eventually extended upward on both ships.

29. BRINNIN, p. 454. "Kitsch" is a derogatory term describing a kind of lowbrow art (to use a highbrow expression). See Gillo Dorfles, *Kitsch: The World of Bad Taste* (New York: Universe Books, 1970).

30. One of which was streamlined!

31. See NEIL POTTER and JACK FROST, *The Queen Mary* (New York: The John Day Co., 1961), pp. 102, 103.

32. The *Queen Mary* has since been stripped of her decor and her insides gutted in the process of converting it to a museum-convention center for Long Beach.

33. EDWIN P. ALEXANDER, *The Pennsylvania Railroad* (New York: W. W. Norton, 1947), p. 135.

34. *Ferry Tales,* vol. I., no. 3 (n.d). A joint publication of the Delaware-New Jersey and the Virginia Ferry companies. Unpaged pamphlet. The *Princess Anne* carried 2,000 passengers.

35. *Ibid.*

36. From a Panama Line pamphlet. Undated, unpaged.

37. From data supplied by the State Ferries Division of the Washington State Dept. of Highways. The *Kalakala* held 70 autos and 1,943 passengers.

38. Note from Mr. Kuhler, Jan. 5, 1975.

## V. FLIGHT BY RAIL: THE STREAMLINED TRAIN

1. Greenough, "American Architecture," in *Form and Function,* ed. Harold Small, p. 58.

2. *Ibid.,* p. 59.

3. SAMUEL R. CALTHROP, *Improvement in Construction of Railway Trains and Cars,* U.S. Patent No. 49,227 (Washington: U.S. Patent Office, Aug. 8, 1865), p. 1. The term "air-resisting" described a form designed to resist the drag effect of air. It is no longer commonly used.

4. *Ibid.,* p. 5.

5. *Ibid.,* p. 2.

6. *Ibid.* Apparently the train was never built.

7. FREDERICK UPHAM ADAMS, *Atmospheric Resistance and Its Relation to the Speed of Trains* (Chicago: Rand, McNally, 1892).

8. DAVID H. HAMLEY and RAYMOND F. CORLEY, "How it All Began—I," *Trains,* vol. XXXIV, no. 1 (November 1973), p. 39.

9. *Ibid.*

10. OTTO KUHLER, "Streamlining, Part I: An Autobiography," *Bulletin of the National Railway Historical Society,* vol. XXXIX, no. 1 (1974), p. 10.

11. *Ibid.*

12. DAVID P. MORGAN, "He Sold Streamlining," *Trains and Travel,* vol. XII, no. 9 (July 1952), p. 15.

13. SHELDON and ARENS, *Consumer Engineering*, p. 41.

14. "Drop of Water Points Way to Higher Speeds," *Popular Mechanics*, vol. LV, no. 6 (June 1931), p. 977.

15. "The Dark Horse of the Rails," *Popular Mechanics*, vol. LV, no. 3 (March 1931), p. 382.

16. LEWIS MUMFORD, *Technics and Civilization* (New York: Harbinger Books, 1963), caption to fig. 4 opposite p. 277.

17. GEDDES, *Horizons*, p. 34.

18. *Ibid.*, p. 77.

19. *Ibid.*

20. *Ibid.*, p. 78.

21. EDWARD HUNGERFORD, *The American Railroad in Laboratory* (Washington: The American Railway Association, 1933), p. 8.

22. *Ibid.*, p. 12.

23. MARTIN D. STEVERS, *Steel Rails: The Epic of the Railroads* (New York: Grosset & Dunlap, 1933), p. 364.

24. "Streamliner—City of Salina," *Info*, vol. III, no. 11 (Sept., Oct. 1971), p. 16.

25. "Union Pacific Installs Light-Weight High-Speed Passenger Train," *Railway Age*, vol. XCVI, no. 5 (Feb. 3, 1934), pp. 186, 187.

26. *Ibid.*, p. 194.

27. "Streamliner—City of Salina," p. 18.

28. TOM BUSACK, "Pioneer Zephyr," *Model Railroader*, vol. XXVI, no. 10 (Oct. 1959), p. 54.

29. PAUL P. CRET, "Streamlined Trains," *Magazine of Art*, vol. XXX, no. 1 (Jan. 1937), p. 19.

30. RKO used the *Pioneer Zephyr* as a set for the 1934 film *The Silver Streak*.

31. Goodyear Tire and Rubber Co., "Comet Brought Fame to Goodyear," *Wingfoot Clan* (Aug. 20, 1964).

32. NORMAN F. ZAPF, "The Streamlining of a Locomotive" (unpublished Bachelor of Science thesis, Case School of Applied Science, 1934). Zapf was provided with information and blueprints by the American Locomotive Company, the Union Pacific and Burlington railroads and his later employer, the New York Central.

33. "The Engineers Praise it Highly," *The Case Alumnus*, vol. XIV, no. 4 (Feb., March, 1935), p. 14.

34. BRIAN REED, *The Hiawathas*, Loco Profile No. 26 (Windsor, Berkshire, England: Profile Publications Ltd., 1972), p. 27. Steam engines are classified by

their wheel arrangement. The "Atlantic" type has four small pilot (front) wheels, four large driving wheels (drivers) and two trailing wheels. Of course only half are visible on either side.

35. *Ibid.,* p. 28.

36. ERIC ARCHER, "Streamlined Steam," *Quadrant Press Review* no. 1 (New York: Quadrant Press, 1972), p. 3.

37. REED, *The Hiawathas,* p. 47.

38. ARCHER, "Streamlined Steam," p. 6.

39. HENRY DREYFUSS, *Designing For People,* p. 122.

40. LAWRENCE W. SAGLE, *A Picture History of B & O Motive Power* (New York: Simmons-Boardman, 1952), pp. 32–34.

41. ARCHER, "Streamlined Steam," p. 17.

42. RAYMOND LOEWY, *The Locomotive: Its Esthetics* (New York: The Studio Publications, Inc., 1937), unpaged.

43. EDWIN P. ALEXANDER, *The Pennsylvania Railroad* (New York: W. W. Norton, 1947), pp. 211–214.

44. BRIAN REED, *New York Central Hudsons,* Loco Profile No. 2 (Windsor, Berkshire, England: Profile Productions Ltd., n.d.), p. 48.

45. Mars, the helmeted allegorical figure of war, can be found in political cartoons of the late 1930s, the eve of the Second World War. The general effect of a shield is suggested by Dreyfuss' engine front, which was designed to "combat" air-resistance.

46. "Power. A Portfolio by Charles Sheeler," *Fortune,* vol. XXII, no. 6 (Dec. 1940), pp. 73–83.

47. LUCIUS BEEBE, *20th Century Limited* (Berkeley, Calif.: Howell-North Books, 1962), p. 158.

48. ARCHER, "Streamlined Steam," p. 6.

49. STAN REPP, "The Story of the Super Chief," *Trains,* vol. XXI, no. 7 (May 1962), p. 33.

50. LOEWY, *The Locomotive: Its Esthetics,* unpaged.

51. REPP, "The Story of the Super Chief," p. 35.

52. CRET, "Streamlined Trains," p. 19.

53. See Repp's article for a reproduction of the *Super Chief's* May 18, 1937 menu, which also featured caviar, hearts of artichokes, fresh asparagus, apricot parfait and English Chesire cheese with guava jelly. Repp reports that passengers wishing trout for dinner the second day placed their orders the first night out. The chef would wire an order ahead to Las Vegas, New Mexico, where fresh-caught trout would be waiting for the train when it arrived.

54. REPP, "The Story of the Super Chief," p. 39.

55. "Another Year of Passenger Progress," *Railway Age,* vol. III, no. 19 (Nov. 22, 1941), p. 816.

56. *Ibid.*

57. "March of the Streamliners," *Railway Age,* vol. III, no. 19 (Nov. 22, 1941), pp. 829–48.

58. ARCHER, "Streamlined Steam," p. 4.

59. BRIAN REED, *Pennsylvania Duplexii,* Loco Profile No. 24 (Windsor, Berkshire, England: Profile Publications, 1972), p. 268.

60. ALEXANDER, *The Pennsylvania Railroad,* p. 175.

61. Editors of *Trains and Travel* magazine, "Streamlined Makeshifts," *Steam Locomotives* (Milwaukee: Kalmbach Publishing Co., 1953), unpaged.

62. EDWIN P. ALEXANDER, *American Locomotives* (New York: Bonanza Books, 1950), p. 204.

63. H. STAFFORD BRYANT, JR., "Ps–4," *Steam Locomotives* (Milwaukee: Kalmbach Publishing Co., 1953), unpaged.

64. CHARLES DICKENS, *Hard Times,* ed. by G. Ford and S. Monod (New York: W. W. Norton, 1966), p. 17.

65. MARK TWAIN (SAMUEL L. CLEMENS), *The Adventures of Huckleberry Finn* (London: J. M. Dent and Sons, 1955), p. 110.

66. FRANK NORRIS, *The Octopus* (Garden City, N.J.: Doubleday, 1947), p. 47.

67. Conversation with Mr. Kuhler, Feb. 13, 1973.

68. ARCHER, p. 34.

69. "Streamliners Now Operate on a Strictly Utilitarian Basis," *Railway Age,* vol. CXV, no. 21 (Nov. 20, 1943), p. 810.

70. *Thirtieth Annual Report of the Board of Supervising Engineers, Chicago Traction Authority* (Chicago: Chicago Traction Authority, 1937), p. 114.

## VI. TERRANAUTICS: THE STREAMLINED AUTOMOBILE

1. GEDDES, *Horizons,* p. 24.

2. *Ibid.,* p. 25.

3. K. G. PONTUS HULTÉN, *The Machine as Seen at the End of the Mechanical Age* (New York: Museum of Modern Art, 1968), p. 46.

4. KARL LUDVIGSEN, "Automobile Aerodynamics: Form and Fashion," *Automobile Quarterly,* vol. VI, no. 2 (Fall 1967), p. 147. Forming the curved glass must have presented a formidable challenge.

5. THEODORE VON KÁRMÁN, *The Wind and Beyond* (Boston: Little, Brown and

Co., 1967), pp. 97, 117. Dr. Hugo Eckner was permitted to build a special Zeppelin in 1924 for the United States in partial payment of war reparations (p. 117). Between 1922 and 1926 Junkers built an aircraft factory in Russia and thereby gained military aircraft experience (p. 120). The Treaty was officially broken in 1935 when Air Marshall Goering publicly announced the existence of the Luftwaffe (p. 216).

6. These were little more than mudguards to protect the large windows but they were of low resistance. See Ludvigsen, p. 148. Von Kármán tried unsuccessfully to interest Fritz von Opel in testing his cars at the Aachen wind tunnels. In retrospect he felt streamlining was useful to race cars but not to ordinary cars (Von Kármán, p. 118).

7. LUDVIGSEN, p. 148.

8. *Ibid.* Drag coefficient is an index of ease of penetration. A high coefficient of 1.25 would be that achieved moving a flat plane broadside to the direction of motion. A low number of 0.08 or so is considered a limit. American production cars range around 0.50. Total aerodynamic drag is also proportional to the frontal area of the vehicle.

9. U.S. Patent No. 1,631,269, dated June 7, 1929.

10. *Ibid.*, p. 1.

11. *Ibid.*

12. *Ibid.*

13. SYLVESTER J. LIDDY, "Streamlined Motor Vehicles," *Scientific American,* vol. CL, no. 4 (April 1934), p. 221.

14. RAYNER BANHAM, *Theory and Design in the First Machine Age,* 2nd ed. (New York: Praeger, 1967), pp. 328, 329.

15. Although other Burney designs were more fully streamlined than that shown in Fig. 92, none achieved the aesthetic level of Fuller's Dymaxion Cars. Perhaps Burney's experience as an aeronautical engineer hindered his artistic development.

16. GEDDES, *Horizons,* pp. 49, 50.

17. *Ibid.*, p. 47.

18. *Ibid.*, p. 50.

19. *Ibid.*, p. 54.

20. *Ibid.*, p. 55.

21. *Ibid.*, pp. 59, 62. The vertical fin served as a fuel tank.

22. LUDVIGSEN, pp. 159, 160.

23. See DR. PAUL E. HEMKE, "Aeronautics at Case," *Case Alumnus,* vol. XII, no. 3 (Dec. 1932), pp. 9, 30, 32, and by the same author, "A Great Field for Study

and Research," *Case Alumnus*, vol. XIII, no. 6 (May–June 1934), pp. 8–11, 26, 28.

24. R. H. HEALD, "Aerodynamic Characteristics of Automobile Models," *Bureau of Standards Journal of Research*, vol. II (Aug. 1933), pp. 285–91. Heald referenced publications (p. 285n.) by nine other researchers who had been investigating automobile aeronautics since 1931, including one by Sir Charles Burney.

25. *Ibid.*, p. 285. The models were suspended from wires near but not on a ground plane. Later methods of including ground effect on eddy currents beneath the car included (1) rolling the model on a treadmill during testing and (2) the image method, where two identical models were tested in an over-and-under arrangement with their wheels touching. See R. H. Heald, "Comparison of the Ground-Plane and Image Methods for Representing Ground Effects in tests on Motor Vehicles," *Bureau of Standards Journal of Research*, vol. XIII (Dec. 1934), pp. 863–70.

26. Models 1, 2 and 3 were tested over a 13-to-60 mph speed range. Models 4, 5 and 6 were of equal frontal area and were tested over a range of 30-to-70 mph. The effects of side winds on the last three models were reported the following year. See R. H. Heald, "Air Forces and Yawing Moments for Three Automobile Models," *Bureau of Standards Journal of Research*, vol. XIII (Dec. 1934), pp. 871–78.

27. FULLER, *Ideas and Integrities*, p. 19.

28. For photos of the test models, see Robert Marks, *The Dymaxion World of Buckminster Fuller* (Carbondale, Ill.: Southern Illinois University Press, 1960), figs. 98–104.

29. FULLER, *Ideas and Integrities*, p. 20.

30. MARKS, *The Dymaxion World*, p. 27.

31. U.S. Patent 2,101,057. Issued Dec. 7, 1937.

32. *Ibid.*, p. 1.

33. MARKS, *The Dymaxion World*, pp. 27, 28.

34. U.S. Patent No. 2,101,057, p. 2. The *Dymaxion Car* was reported to have a fuel consumption of 40 miles per gallon. See T. J. Maloney, "Tomorrow's Transportation," *Review of Reviews and World's Work*, vol. LXXXVIII, no. 4 (Oct. 1933), p. 23.

35. The 19-foot *Dymaxion Car* could turn on an 11-foot, 9-inch circle while a standard 14-foot conventional car of 1933 required a 41-foot circle.

36. "The First Dymaxion Transport Unit," *The Architectural Record*, vol. LXXIV, no. 2 (Aug. 1933), p. 147.

37. MARKS, *The Dymaxion World*, pp. 31, 32. A member of the Society of Automotive Engineers noted the tendency of rear-wheel steering to "fishtail," i.e., when the driver steers the front away from an oncoming car, he actually steers

the rear end closer to it. See E. Paul du Pont, "Streamline," *The American Mercury,* vol. XXX, no. 120 (Dec. 1933), p. 502.

38. HUGH KENNER, *Bucky: A Guided Tour of Buckminster Fuller* (New York: William Morrow and Co., 1973), p. 215.

39. *Webster's Biographical Dictionary,* ed. Wm. A. Neilson (Springfield, Mass.: G. & C. Merriam Co., 1953), p. 1,419.

40. WILLIAM B. STOUT, "The New Terranautics," *Scientific American,* vol. CL, no. 3 (March 1934), p. 126.

41. "Stout Announces New Type Automobile," *Scientific American,* vol. CLII, no. 3 (March 1935), p. 152.

42. "An entirely new type automobile," *Design,* vol. XXXVII, no. 2 (June 1935), pp. 39, 40. Thought to resemble the Egyptian beetle, the Scarab was designed for convenience and roadability rather than to satisfy wind-tunnel criteria. Like other radical cars of the decade, it never saw mass production.

43. "Car of the Future Session, Annual Meeting," *SAE Journal,* vol. XXXVIII, no. 2 (Feb. 1936), pp. 51, 52. Stout's attitudes about the streamlined car and his Scarab design of 1935 must be considered in light of the appearance of the highly publicized 1934 Chrysler *Airflow* as well as the *Dymaxion Cars.*

44. LUDVIGSEN, pp. 150, 151.

45. "Another Teardrop," *Scientific American,* vol. CLVII, no. 6 (Dec. 1937), p. 376. One suspects the vehicle would have been dangerously overloaded at the front.

46. TEAGUE, *Design This Day,* p. 178.

47. "Jeep" stood for G. P. or General Purpose Vehicle.

48. CHARLES BONVER, JR., "The Patrician Among Coaches," *Arts and Decoration,* vol. XVIII, no. 4 (Feb. 1923), p. 31.

49. *Ibid.,* p. 67.

50. JANE HEAP, "Machine-Age Exposition," Catalogue of the Exposition, unserialized supplement to *The Little Review,* vol. XI (1927), p. 37.

51. JOHN H. YZENBAARD, "A Detroit Hallmark: Body by Dietrich," *Detroit in Perspective: A Journal of Regional History,* vol. 1, no. 2 (Winter 1973), p. 147. The LeBaron company was later absorbed by the Briggs Manufacturing Company which, in turn, became part of the Chrysler Corporation. The name "LeBaron" still appears on some Chrysler models.

52. Cars built before 1925 or so are classified as *antiques.* Those built thereafter and until World War II are called *classic cars.* Interview with Mr. Dietrich, Jan. 3, 1975.

53. "The Story of GM Styling," a General Motors press release, dated Nov. 5, 1962, p. 1.

54. *Ibid.,* p. 2.

55. The danger of this necessary procedure was illustrated by the *Edsel*, named after Henry Ford's son. During the development period, the market for a moderately expensive larger car disappeared and the public opted for the new small compacts developed to compete with foreign cars.

56. Technical Information Department, Chrysler Corp. Engineering Office, *Story of the Airflow Cars*, 1934–1937 (Detroit: Chrysler Corp., 1963), p. 6.

57. *Ibid.*, p. 1.

58. ALEXANDER KLEMIN, "How Research Makes Possible the Modern Motor Car," *Scientific American*, vol. CLI, no. 2 (Aug. 1934), p. 62.

59. "New Airflow Chrysler," *Fortune*, vol. IX, no. 3 (March 1934), p. 17.

60. *Ibid.*

61. *Fortune*, vol. IX, no. 6 (June 1934), p. 39; and vol. IX, no. 4 (April 1934), p. 13.

62. The Chrysler *Airflows* were in the higher 1934 price ranges. The Eight sold for $1,245 and the Imperial for $1,495. By comparison, the conventional Chrysler Six began at $725, and a Plymouth could be had for $530.

63. DREYFUSS, p. 68. E. L. Cord had predicted in 1929 that a perfectly designed streamlined body would be so "futuristic" that few motorists would care to buy it. See "More Speed," *Popular Mechanics*, vol. 51, no. 3 (March 1929), p. 372.

64. HENRY CRANE, "The Car of the Future," *SAE Journal*, vol. XLIV, no. 4 (April 1939), p. 142.

65. B. P. B. DE DUBÉ, "Tatra, The Constant Czech," *Automobile Quarterly*, vol. VII, no. 3 (Winter 1969), p. 311.

66. WALTER HENRY NELSON, *Small Wonder: The Amazing Story of the Volkswagen*, rev. ed. (Boston: Little, Brown and Co., 1967), pp. 46, 47.

VII. ARCHITECTURE: THE STREAMLINED MODERNE

1. RICHARD BUCKMINSTER FULLER, *4D Time Lock*, p. 6. Fuller mailed mimeographed copies of his original 1927 proposal to a number of prominent individuals and included their responses in the 1928 and later editions of *4D Time Lock*.

2. *Ibid.*, pp. 4, 5.

3. *Ibid.*, pp. 1–3.

4. Fuller's six-panel drawing of 1927 shows a Zeppelin dropping a bomb and then "planting" the apartment building into the excavation.

5. The Bureau of Standards conducted wind-tunnel tests on models of buildings as well as autos.

6. The units were contracted by the Air Force, later resold to Fuller's project and are now part of a private home. As with other of Fuller's projects, the cost of tooling up for production discouraged further development.

7. Bureau of Reclamation, *Sculptures at Hoover Dam* (Washington: U. S. Gov't. Printing Office, 1968), p. 8.

8. NORMAN BEL GEDDES, "The House of Tomorrow," *Ladies' Home Journal*, vol. 48, no. 4 (April 1931), p. 12.

9. A cutaway view revealed two conventional boxy autos in the garage. Although Geddes was already designing "teardrop" cars he may have felt their appearance in the drawing would suggest the house was meant for the *distant* future which was not his intent.

10. *Ibid.* A 1936 article in *The Architectural Forum* urged that the improvements wrought in industrial design be emulated in domestic architecture. In it the writer called the New York Central's *Mercury* "more than a streamlined train. It is a clear statement of the possibilities in train design, exhibiting a high order of constructive imagination. . . . Exigencies of machine production are not yet as great in building designs as in trains, electric irons, and frying pans. There can be no doubt, however, that a public accustomed to traveling in such trains as the 'Mercury' will soon begin to wonder about its houses." See "The Mercury," *The Architectural Forum*, vol. LV, no. 2 (Aug. 1936), p. 119.

11. Geddes's ideas were generally consistent with those of the modern European movements. See Banham, *Theory and Design*, pp. 88–97.

12. The Scottish architect Charles Rennie Mackintosh designed built-in furniture for the bedroom of the Hill House in 1902–03 in order to unify the room. Another designer of the Art Nouveau period, Richard Riemerschmid, created a music room for the 1899 German Art Exhibition in Dresden in which a large table was not a separate element but was "absorbed" into a wide windowsill; the transition was made by large hyperbolic curves. Henri Van de Velde designed four rooms for Samuel Bing's shop, L'Art Nouveau, in 1895. The critic Edmond de Goncourt labeled the designs "Yachting Style," acknowledging their semblance to ships' interiors where safety and space requirements demand compact, integrated furnishings, with rounded corners.

13. In rounding the edges below the vanity, Geddes doubtless had the welfare of the lady in mind. Both Frank Lloyd Wright and Gerrit Rietveld complained of having bruised their ankles on angular furniture they had designed.

14. In 1869 Harriet Beecher Stowe and her sister, Catherine Beecher, published *The American Woman's Home.* They felt that in a democratic society the use of servants should be minimal and they promoted small, compact and simple domestic establishments. Their kitchen design featured a continuous working surface and conveniently arranged built-in storage units, an early forerunner of the efficient, streamlined kitchens of the 1930s. See Siegfried Giedion, *Mechanization Takes Command* (New York: W. W. Norton, 1969), pp. 515–17.

15. For a complete account of the *Dymaxion* bathroom's history see Marks, *The Dymaxion World*, pp. 34, 35. The Pullman Company was also engaged in, and had pioneered, the development of compact plumbing units.

16. Due to shortages the *Tower* was constructed primarily of brick with a coating of stucco. Albert Einstein, for whom the *Tower* was named, summed up his impression of it in a single word: "organic."

17. The building combined an observatory and an astrophysical laboratory in which spectro-analytical phenomena would be investigated in relation to Einstein's Theory of Relativity.

18. ALDOUS HUXLEY, "Puritanism in Art," *Creative Art,* vol. VI, no. 3 (March 1930), p. 201.

19. Mooser's father, designer of nearby Ghirardelli Square, was involved in the construction of the Casino.

20. From materials supplied by the Maritime Museum, San Francisco.

21. Plans to heat the lagoon with the discharge of a Pacific Gas and Electric plant never came to fruition.

22. The Coke bottle has an organic form suited to the Streamlined Moderne style. The pinch-waisted version of the bottle was created in 1915 by employees of the Root Glass Company of Terre Haute, Indiana. Alex Samuelson and T. Clyde Edwards gave it its final shape.

23. REYNER BANHAM, *Los Angeles: The Architecture of Four Ecologies* (Harmondsworth, England: Penguin Books, 1973), p. 132.

24. KATHLEEN CHURCH PLUMMER, "The Streamlined Moderne," *Art in America,* vol. 62, no. 1 (Jan.–Feb. 1974), pp. 46–54.

25. *Ibid.,* pp. 46, 47.

26. "Things to Come," *The Architectural Forum,* vol. LXIV, no. 5 (May 1936), p. 421.

27. On an international level our professed isolationism provided an escapist and illusionary insulation from world problems.

28. For Buck, getting there was half the fun. In his analysis of Depression-era comics, Dr. Young sees the futuristic city as an image of harmony and orderliness and Buck's vehicles and weapons as technological means of overcoming difficulties with force. See: William Henry Young, "Images of Order: American Comic Strips During the Depression, 1929–1938" (unpublished doctoral dissertation, Emory Univ., 1969), pp. 189–92.

## VIII. THE WORLD OF TOMORROW

1. GROVER WHALEN, "Story for Everyman," *World's Fair Bulletin,* Theme Edition, vol. 1, no. 2 (Nov. 1936), p. 1. The Fair had a secondary theme: the 150th anniversary of George Washington's inauguration. A 150-foot statue of the first President provided a fitting tribute, but the Fair is remembered for its future-minded theme.

A second world's fair was constructed in 1939 on San Francisco's Treasure Island. The "California International World's Fair on San Francisco Bay" celebrated the completion of the Golden Gate and San Francisco–Oakland Bay bridges and the establishment of an airport and water base for Trans-Pacific *Clipper* planes. The style of the buildings was Zigzag Moderne with stair-stepped towers and overtones of Asian, Polynesian and other Pacific cultures.

2. The word *Trylon* combined tri (three-sided) and pylon. *Perisphere* was an amalgam of peri (beyond, all-around) and sphere. The forms were distilled by architects Harrison and Fouilboux from a thousand sketches; their geometrical simplicity was to "strike a new note in design."

3. *Official Guide Book, New York World's Fair, 1939* (New York: Exposition Publications, 1939), p. 27.

4. Quoted in Siegfried Giedion, "Can Expositions Survive?" *Architectural Forum*, vol. LIX, no. 6 (Dec. 1938), "Plus" section, p. 7.

5. The author enjoyed an updated version of the pageant which Hungerford staged for the 1949 Railroad Fair in Chicago. Both necessitated elaborate switching yards offstage and a half-dozen tracks across the stage.

6. "New York's Fair," *Architectural Forum*, vol. LXIV, no. 6 (June 1936), supplement, p. 9.

7. A survey taken among Fair visitors by George Gallup's American Institute of Public Opinion showed the GM exhibit far outranked all others in popularity. From a GM press release of May 30, 1939.

8. From the Futurama narration script.

9. Futurama was designed by Geddes; George Wittbold supervised its construction. The architectural consultant was Albert Kahn.

10. Futurama narration script.

11. *Ibid.* Geddes had created a smaller "City of Tomorrow" in 1937 as part of a Shell Oil Co. advertising campaign.

12. NORMAN BEL GEDDES, *Magic Motorways* (New York: Random House, 1940), p. 10.

13. *Ibid.*, pp. 3, 4.

14. *Ibid.*

15. *Official Guide Book*, p. 161.

16. *Ibid.*

17. The Westinghouse Electric and Manufacturing Co., *The Time Capsule* (New York: Westinghouse Co., 1933), p. 15.

18. *Ibid.*, p. 9.

19. JOHN MCANDREW, "A Design Student's Guide to the New York World's Fair," *PM*, vol. V, no. 2 (Aug.–Sept., 1939), p. 44.

20. "The New York Fair," *The Architectural Forum*, vol. LXX, no. 6 (June 1939), p. 395.

21. *Ibid.*, p. 397.

## IX. DYNAMIC CONTINUUMS

1. EDWARD ROBERT DE ZURKO, *Origins of Functionalist Theory* (New York: Columbia Univ. Press, 1957), p. 17.

2. Plato: *Philebus*, 51c.

3. S. W. FRANKL, "Platonic Precepts," *The Art News*, vol. XXXII, no. 3 (April 28, 1934), p. 10.

4. The Museum of Modern Art regained its momentum at the end of the decade when it sponsored a competitive exhibition entitled *Organic Design in Home Furnishings* in 1941. Fluid lines and plastic materials were more in evidence at this exhibit. Among the distinguished designs on display was a prize-winning chair in molded plywood by Charles Eames and Eero Saarinen.

5. Later, newer materials and techniques made possible high-pressure injection molding of sharp-edged forms.

6. LASZLO MOHOLY-NAGY, *Vision in Motion* (Chicago: Paul Theobald and Co., 1956), p. 34.

7. DREYFUSS, *Designing for People*, p. 77. See also Eugene Schoen, "Industrial Design: A New Profession," *Magazine of Art*, vol. XXXI, no. 8 (August 1938), p. 475, and Serge Chermayeff and Rene D'Harnoncourt, "Design for Use," *Art in Progress*, ed. by the staff of the Museum of Modern Art (New York: The Museum of Modern Art, 1944), p. 195. The attribution of the pencil sharpener is obscure; apparently its designer hesitates to take credit for it after the controversy.

8. GIEDION, *Mechanization Takes Command*, p. 610.

9. The attention to forms that penetrate suggests the possibility of a subconscious sexual meaning in streamlined forms. Such references can be found in Brancusi's sculpture, and Freud interpreted the Zeppelin as a symbol of the male principle in dreams.

10. See Robert Humphrey's *Stream of Consciousness in the Modern Novel* (Berkeley: The Univ. of California Press, 1962). Humphrey feels this type of novel is identified by its subject matter rather than the technique itself and excludes purely reminiscent works like Marcel Proust's *A la Recherche du Temps Perdue* in favor of works which feature the prespeech levels of consciousness.

11. Humphrey centers his examination on Joyce's *Ulysses* (1922), Woolf's *Mrs. Dalloway* (1925) and *To the Lighthouse* (1927), and Faulkner's *The Sound and the Fury* (1929) and *As I Lay Dying* (1930).

12. WILLIAM JAMES, *Psychology* (Cleveland: World Publishing Co., 1948), p. 159. (A reprint of the 1892 abridgement of *The Principles of Psychology*.)

13. *Ibid.*, p. 160.

14. *Ibid.*, James's discussion concerned the adult consciousness.

15. *Ibid.*, p. 171.

16. *Ibid.*, p. 172.

17. *Ibid.*, p. 261.

18. *Ibid.*, p. 256. Joyce's characters in *Ulysses* make associations from one object to the next. See Humphrey, pp. 26–30.

19. HENRI BERGSON, "Creative Evolution" (1907), trans. Arthur Mitchell, *Selections from Bergson,* ed. Harold A. Larrabee (New York: Appleton-Century-Crofts, 1949), pp. 58, 59.

20. *Ibid.*, p. 59.

21. JOHN DEWEY, *Art and Experience* (New York: Minton, Balch and Co., 1934), p. 36.

22. FRANK B. GILBRETH and LILLIAN M. GILBRETH, *Applied Motion Study* (Easton: Hive Publishing Co., 1973), p. 67.

23. *Ibid.*, p. 68. The flash was intense at the beginning and dim toward the end of each pulse. These appeared as teardrops of light that indicated the direction of the movement.

24. Quoted in Giedion, *Mechanization Takes Command,* p. 102.

25. GILBRETH, p. 89.

26. JOHN A. KOUWENHOVEN, *The Beer Can by the Highway* (Garden City, N.Y.: Doubleday, 1961), p. 42.

# *f*ELECTED
# BIBLIOGRAPHY

ADAMS, FREDERICK UPHAM. *Atmospheric Resistance and Its Relation to the Speed of Trains*. Chicago: Rand, McNally and Co., 1892.

ALEXANDER, EDWIN P. *The Pennsylvania Railroad*. New York: W. W. Norton & Co., 1947.

ALLEN, FREDERICK LEWIS. *Since Yesterday*. New York: Harper and Row, 1972.

ARCHER, ERIC H. *Streamlined Steam*. New York: Quadrant Press, 1972.

BANHAM, REYNER. *Los Angeles: The Architecture of Four Ecologies*. Harmondsworth, England: Penguin, 1973.

————. *Theory and Design in the First Machine Age*. 2nd ed. New York: Praeger, 1967.

BERGSON, HENRI. "Creative Evolution" (1907), trans. by Arthur Mitchell, *Selections from Bergson*, ed. Harold A. Larrabee. New York: Appleton-Century-Crofts, 1949.

BRINNIN, JOHN MALCOLM. *The Sway of the Grand Saloon*. New York: Delacorte Press, 1971.

CHENEY, SELDON and MARTHA CHENEY. *Art and the Machine*. New York: Whittlesey House, 1936.

DAVIES, R. E. G. "Pan Am's Planes," *Air Pictorial*, Part 1, vol. 29, no. 9 (Sept.,1967), p. 2–6; Part 2, vol. 29, no. 10 (Oct.,1967), pp. 8–12.

DEWEY, JOHN. *Art and Experience*. New York: Minton, Balch and Co., 1934.

DREYFUSS, HENRY. *Designing for People*. New York: Simon and Schuster, 1955.

FULLER, RICHARD BUCKMINSTER. *4D Time Lock*. Corrales, N.M.: Lama Foundation, 1970.

———. *Ideas and Integrities*, ed. Robert W. Marks. New York: Collier Books, 1969.

———. *Nine Chains to the Moon*. Carbondale, Ill.: Southern Illinois Univ. Press, 1963.

GEDDES, NORMAN BEL. *Horizons*. New York: Random House, 1932.

———. "The House of Tomorrow," *Ladies' Home Journal*, vol. 48, no. 4 (April, 1931), pp. 12, 13, 162.

———. *Magic Motorways*. New York: Random House, 1940.

———. "Streamlining," *The Atlantic Monthly*, vol. 154, no. 5 (Nov.,1934), pp. 553–563.

GIACOMELLI, R. and E. PISTOLESI. "Historical Sketch," *Aerodynamic Theory: A General Review of Progress*, ed. Wm. F. Durand. New York: Dover, 1963. Vol. 1, pp. 305–394.

GIBBS-SMITH, CHARLES H. *Sir George Cayley's Aeronautics, 1796–1855*. London: H.M.S.O., 1962.

GIEDION, SIEGFRIED. *Mechanization Takes Command*. New York: W. W. Norton and Co., Inc., 1969.

HUMPHREY, ROBERT. *Stream of Consciousness in the Modern Novel*. Berkeley: The Univ. of Calif. Press, 1962.

JAMES, WILLIAM. *Psychology*. Cleveland: World Publishing Co., 1948.

KUHLER, OTTO. *My Iron Journey: An Autobiography of a Life with Steam and Steel*. Denver: Intermountain Chapter, National Railway Hist. Soc., 1967.

———. "Streamlining," *Bulletin, Nat. Railway Hist. Soc.*, vol. 39, no. 1 (1974), pp. 7–15, 22–24.

LE CORBUSIER (CHARLES EDOUARD JEANNERET). *Aircraft*. New York: The Studio Publications, 1935.

———. *Towards a New Architecture*. New York: Praeger, 1960.

LOEWY, RAYMOND. *The Locomotive: Its Esthetics*. New York: The Studio Publications, 1937.

———. *Never Leave Well Enough Alone*. New York: Simon and Schuster, 1951.

LUDVIGSEN, KARL. "Automobile Aerodynamics: Form and Fashion," *Automobile Quarterly*, vol. 6, no. 2 (Fall, 1967), pp. 146–165.

MARKS, ROBERT. *The Dymaxion World of Buckminster Fuller*. Carbondale, Ill.: Southern Ill. Univ. Press, 1960.

MAXTONE-GRAHAM, JOHN. *The Only Way to Cross*. New York: Macmillan, 1972.

PLUMMER, KATHLEEN CHURCH. "The Streamlined Moderne," *Art in America*, vol. 62, no. 1 (Jan.,Feb.,1974), pp. 46–54.

POTTER, NEIL and JACK FROST. *The Queen Mary*. New York: John Day, 1961.

RANDERS-PEHRSON, N. H. "Pioneer Wind Tunnels," *Smithsonian Miscellaneous Collection*, vol. 93, no. 4 (Jan.,1935), pp. 1–14.

REED, BRIAN. *The Hiawathas*, Loco Profile no. 26. Windsor, Berkshire, England: Profile Publications, 1972.

————. *New York Central Hudsons,* Loco Profile no. 2. Windsor, Berkshire, England: Profile Productions, Ltd., n.d.

————. *Pennsylvania Duplexii,* Loco Profile no. 24. Windsor, Berkshire, England: Profile Publications, 1972.

REPP, STAN. "The Story of the Super Chief," *Trains,* vol. 21, no. 7 (May,1962), pp. 30–41.

ROBB, A. M. "The Development of Applied Hydrodynamics," *A History of Technology: The Late Nineteenth Century,* ed. C. Singer et al. Oxford: Clarendon Press, 1958. Vol. 5, pp. 386–390.

SHAPIRO, ASCHER H. *Shape and Flow: The Fluid Dynamics of Drag.* Garden City, N.Y.: Anchor Books, 1961.

SHELDON, ROY and EGMONT ARENS. *Consumer Engineering: A New Technique for Prosperity.* New York: Harper and Bros., 1932.

TEAGUE, WALTER DORWIN. *Design This Day: The Technique of Order in the Machine Age.* New York: Harcourt, Brace and Co., 1940.

THOMPSON, SIR D'ARCY WENTWORTH. *On Growth and Form.* 2 vols. 2nd ed. reprinted. Cambridge: Syndics of the Cambridge Univ. Press, 1963.

VON KÁRMÁN, THEODORE. *Aerodynamics: Selected Topics in the Light of Their Historical Development.* Ithaca: Cornell Univ. Press, 1954.

————. *The Wind and Beyond.* Boston: Little, Brown and Co., 1967.

WESTINGHOUSE ELECTRIC and MANUFACTURING CO. *The Time Capsule.* New York: Westinghouse, 1938.

ZAPF, NORMAN F. "The Streamlining of a Locomotive." Unpublished Bachelor of Science thesis. Cleveland: Case School of Applied Science, 1934.

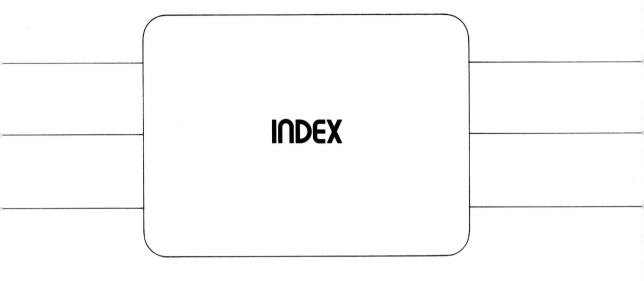

# INDEX

Boldfaced numbers refer to Figure numbers.

211